But I'm Not a Reading Teacher:

Strategies for Literacy Instruction in the Content Areas

Amy Benjamin

EYE ON EDUCATION
6 DEPOT WAY WEST, SUITE 106
LARCHMONT, NY 10538
(914) 833–0551
(914) 833–0761 fax
www.eyeoneducation.com

Library of Congress Cataloging-in-Publication Data

Benjamin, Amy, 1951-
But I'm not a reading teacher : strategies for literacy instruction in the content
areas / Amy Benjamin.
       p. cm.
    ISBN 1-59667-049-5
1. Content area reading—Handbooks, manuals, etc. 2. Language arts—Correla-
tion with content subjects—Handbooks, manuals, etc. I. Title.
LB1050.455.B46 2007
428.4071'2—dc22

                                              2007011675

10 9 8 7 6 5 4 3 2

Editorial and production services provided by
Richard H. Adin Freelance Editorial Services
52 Oakwood Blvd., Poughkeepsie, NY 12603-4112
(845-471-3566)

Also Available from EYE ON EDUCATION

Active Literacy Across the Curriculum:
Strategies for Reading, Writing, Speaking, and Listening
Heidi Hayes Jacobs

Writing in the Content Areas, 2nd Edition
Amy Benjamin

Writing Put to the Test:
Teaching for the High-Stakes Essay
Amy Benjamin

Differentiated Instruction:
A Guide for Middle and High School Teachers
Amy Benjamin

Differentiated Instruction:
A Guide for Elementary Teachers
Amy Benjamin

Socratic Seminars and Literature Circles
for Middle and High School English
Victor and Marc Moeller

What Great Teachers Do *Differently*:
14 Things that Matter Most
Todd Whitaker

Seven Simple Secrets:
What the Best Teachers Know and Do
Annette Breaux and Todd Whitaker

Classroom Motivation From A to Z:
How to Engage Your Students in Learning
Barbara Blackburn

Handbook on Differentiated Instruction
for Middle and High Schools
Sheryn Spencer Northey

Reading, Writing and Gender:
Instructional Strategies and Activities
That Work for Girls and Boys
Gail Goldberg and Barbara Roswell

Acknowledgments

I would like to express my appreciation to Peggy Daisey, David Johns, Pam Ours, and Catherine Thome. Their thoughtful commentary on this book when it was a work in progress was extremely helpful. I am grateful once again to my publisher, Robert N. Sickles, for encouraging me to create this vision of how secondary-school teachers can improve their students' performance through better reading comprehension.

Meet the Author

Amy Benjamin, a veteran English teacher, trains educators throughout the country in writing across the curriculum, strategic literacy, and differentiated instruction. She has received awards for excellence in teaching from the New York State English Council, Tufts University, and Union College. As president of the Assembly for the Teaching of English Grammar, an affiliate of the National Council of Teachers of English, she is a leading authority on effective ways to teach both academic and creative writing. She is the author of eight books.

How to Use This Book

This book gives content area teachers specific examples of text, tests, mini-lessons, strategies, and points of difficulty in the various subjects in secondary school. To help you locate information that is particularly applicable for the subject that you teach, we've provided visual cues:

This symbol signifies actual text of the kind that the student would be reading in your class.

This symbol signifies reading material that would be in a test in a given subject area.

In addition, as you read, you'll notice marginal tabs that help you find information that is directly relevant to domain-specific reading comprehension strategies.

I've divided the book into four parts:

Part One, "About Academic Reading" explains what you need to know about the role that reading plays in learning beyond the elementary level, the expectations that our students face, and their need to be prepared to meet our expectations for information processing. The information that they need to understand, analyze, synthesize, and apply comes from listening in class as well as reading, but reading and listening must go together if students are to process and eventually "own" information.

Part Two explains the different demands and features of subject area, also called "domain-specific" or "genre-specific" reading. It is important that you know how what you are asking your students to read requires skills that are significantly different from those in the students' other classes.

Part Three presents research-based strategies that improve reading comprehension. As you read these, you might find yourself thinking: "These are strategies that apply not only to reading, but to listening to a lecture." That is the point: Reading comprehension is information processing, but the information is delivered through the symbolic, abstract system of encoded visual cues on a page. I've divided the strategies into those that are effective *before* reading, those that are to be used *during* reading, and those that readers use *after* the reading is done to integrate new knowledge into existing networks of knowledge.

Part Four is more global in scope, evaluating school-wide structures and interventions that aim to improve reading comprehension, particularly for deficit readers. If you think that "the reading problems" can be fixed by simply hiring a specialist and setting up remediation, then I suggest that you consider what recent research has to say on the reading specialist's role and limitations. Fact is, an accumulating body of evidence suggests that the reading specialist's most effective role on the secondary level is to work with *you* in the capacity of a literacy coach, rather than to work with students in an isolated reading lab on individual reading skills. Finally, I've added a simple graphic organizer for strategic reading that is designed to help students develop the habits of mind to prepare for, attend to, and reflect upon a reading task.

Table of Contents

I

About
Academic Reading

1

Learning and Reading

I've grounded the teaching suggestions in this book in certain pedagogical principles that are supported by research (Jensen, Caine and Caine, Fogarty) and that I can personally endorse based on more than three decades as an English teacher and literacy coach.

First, we learn:

- ◆ Information in layers, over time
- ◆ Information best when we organize it into patterns
- ◆ Information best when we gather it into clusters
- ◆ Through our senses
- ◆ Through socialization
- ◆ Through prompts, cues, and associations

Second, learning is:

- ◆ Natural. Reading is artificial. To learn through reading, our energies have to be focused on comprehension, not the artificial act of decoding, which has to be automatic.

- ◆ Habitual. We tend to gravitate toward certain modes of receiving, processing, and remembering information.

- ◆ Cumulative. The more we know, the more we are capable of learning. The more sophisticated learning becomes, the more it depends on prior knowledge.

All of the research about durable learning supports these tent-post learning principles. Here is a brief explanation of them and how they relate specifically to reading comprehension.

We learn in layers, over time. What this means is that we learn by connecting new knowledge into an existing structure of what we can call *old* knowledge. We do not learn a lot of information all at once. The mind is not like a computer, accepting a CD full of information. The mind learns in layers, in a manner not unlike the way paint is applied to wood: The wood soaks up the first coat, and *then* is ready to accept more coats. This is why we have the metaphor of the *learning curve*.

3

We learn in patterns. Educational researchers Renate Nummela Caine and Geoffrey Caine assert that learning in patterns is a key principle in how the brain makes sense of information. Conversely, the brain, resisting chaos and meaninglessness, actively imposes order by creating patterns: "(the brain) resists having meaninglessness imposed on it. Really effective education must give learners an opportunity to formulate their own patterns of understanding." I see two kinds of instructional implications of the pattern-learning principle that relate to reading comprehension. The first is the use of graphic organizers to make sense of text, to turn it into a pattern. The second, used along with the first, is that text itself forms patterns: narrative, description, classification, cause and effect, comparison-contrast, definition, exemplification, and process analysis. As we read, we can improve comprehension by perceiving that the text is written primarily in one of these patterns. We can then use an appropriate graphic organizer to see how the pattern holds the meaning.

We learn through our senses. Information that has come in through the senses tends to be memorable. Information that has come in through more than one sense tends to be even more memorable. Instructional implications of the sensory learning principle as it relates to reading comprehension involve creating sensory input, encouraging the imagining of sensory input during reading, and limiting extraneous sensory input during reading. We can accomplish the first by reading aloud, providing visuals and encouraging the use of existing visuals in the text as a reading comprehension aid, using color-coding as a memory aid. We should remind readers to visualize vividly as they read and to draw pictures or graphic organizers that represent what was read. We should instill the meaning-making habit of asking questions during reading that evoke sensory input: *What did you see in the text? What did you hear? What textures did you feel?* And, don't overlook the importance of instilling the habit of reading without extraneous noise and distractions whenever possible.

We learn through socialization. How many times have you come to understand something by talking it through with someone else? Socialization is a powerful, authentic learning force, often overlooked as a reading comprehension aid because reading is thought of as a solitary process. Reading itself can be solitary, but making meaning out of reading need not be. The instructional implications of socializing reading comprehension are that we can set up reading partnerships where readers question each other to achieve comprehension. Readers can work on a post-reading activity that gives them the opportunity to mesh minds to fill in gaps in understanding. And working with a reading partner is motivational: Someone else is depending on you to read and help them understand.

We learn through prompts, cues, and association. Think about what happens when you *remind yourself* of something. What triggered the reminder? It happens all the time: A stimulus sets off a chain that leads you straight to something else. That is how the cuing system of the brain works. Because the brain has its own efficient cuing mechanism, we need to harness its energy as a reading comprehension tool. Educational psychologists speak of *chunking* as the way in which the mind can treat a cluster of related information as if it were a unit. The ability to chunk information is extremely important for effective learning management. The short-term memory is capable of holding only a handful of unrelated bits of information, as you know it you've ever tried to remember a phone number for more than a few seconds. But when you put the numbers into clusters, chunking them, you can hold more information in short-term memory, and later in long-term memory, should you decide to file that phone number in your mental directory. The instructional implication for reading comprehension is that we need to instill the habit of reading phrases as units of meaning, rather than reading single words. Single word reading is very inefficient, and it characterizes the way deficit readers approach text.

Learning is natural. Reading is artificial. The brain knows how to learn, wants to learn, loves to learn. Learning through language is perhaps the most natural form of learning of all, certainly the most human. That textbook is full of information that will help the world seem more satisfying to its readers. So if learning is so natural, why do so many of our students resist it so much, especially when the learning is locked up in text? Reading is artificial. It is an abstract, symbolic system having all kinds of encoded signals that don't exist in speech (punctuation, spelling, many non–speech-like syntactical arrangements of words). Not only that, but a reader can't be doing what humans naturally want to do: jump around, let our minds run free, watch television, eat, and so on. To read and actually get something out of it, the reader has to turn his or her brain over to an unseen author and allow the message of that offer, a message offered in code, to become its primary focus, forsaking all other thoughts that would lead the brain elsewhere. Not only that, but simultaneously, the reader must be aware of lapses and get back on track, usually by rereading. That any reading at all ever gets done is a wonder when you consider what the body and brain would really rather be doing! Fortunately, learning, I remind you, is natural, and I think it's safe to say that everybody would *like* to become better readers, especially if they could do so with minimal effort, and if being better readers meant also being *faster* readers. The instructional implication of the natural tension that exists between wanting to learn and wanting to read is that these two fighting forces must cozy up to each other. The *I Want to Learn Brain* must break down the resistance of the *I Don't Want to Read Brain*. One way for this to happen is that we must understand the abstract nature of reading and then make the reading experience more concrete. This happens through visualization. When you read the words "the apple," you are seeing ink, not an apple. So you must visualize the apple, concretize the abstract.

Learning is habitual. The more we practice a process, the more its steps become automatic. This happy circumstance means that consistency and persistence in teaching the reading strategies will pay off. Educational psychologists distinguish two kinds of learning: memory learning and habit learning. The former is about amassing facts and figures; the latter is about developing behaviors that become ingrained after continual reinforcement. Students who learn that reading is a process with pre-, during, and post-reading steps will eventually internalize that process, giving themselves what they need to maximize comprehension. But, that won't happen by being told what to do alone: They need guided practice and monitored opportunities to use the strategies.

Learning is cumulative. Reading comprehension depends heavily on prior knowledge about the subject. It may seem too obvious to deserve mention, but the more we know about a subject, the easier it is to read new information about it. This is not only because of the principle that we learn in layers, but also because every subject has its own language and much of this language is metaphor, jargon, allusion, abbreviations, and acronyms. Learning is like investment capital: The more learning (wealth) you have, the more you can use that knowledge (wealth) to create more. Pick up any bit of text, and you'll see how much prior knowledge, general and domain-specific, is necessary to read it for meaning. Reading for meaning goes way beyond knowing what the individual words mean: What do the words mean *as used in that context?* The instructional implication is that any kind of reading is good reading if it contributes to the reader's knowledge base and increases the reader's stamina for reading.

Problem-solvers connect the dots. What all of these learning principles have been leading up to is that problem-solvers make meaning by putting together what they already know with new information. We know that we make sense of the world by connecting the dots. What we need to know for our students' sakes is that *we need a lot of dots!* Where do we get them? We get dots from our education, experience, cultural activities, and social interactions. Dots accumulate language. Language is the stuff of reading. Anytime a student leaves your classroom knowing something about this great big world of ours, you have made that student more capable of being a great reader!

Anatomy of a Definition of Reading

Here is how the National Council of Teachers of English (NCTE) defines reading:

> "Reading is a complex, purposeful, social and cognitive process in which readers simultaneously use their knowledge of spoken and written language, their knowledge of the topic of the text, and their knowledge of their culture to construct meaning. Reading is not a technical skill acquired once and for all in the primary grades, but rather a developmental process. A reader's competence continues to grow through engagement with various types of texts and wide reading for various purposes over a lifetime" (NCTE, 2006).

Let's unpack this important conceptual definition to see its instructional implications. First, let's look at those four adjectives that inform our definition of what reading (comprehension) is: complex, purposeful, social, and cognitive.

Complex process: That reading is a *complex process* implies that many strategies must be folded into it and that it (comprehension) results from multiple paths to the brain. The complexity of the reading process refers also to the fact that comprehension results from the reader's emotions, cognition, motivation, ambient physical conditions (lighting, noise, visuals, comfort), and experience.

Purposeful process: That reading is a *purposeful process* implies that the reader, like a hunter, should be knowing what to look for and, accordingly, should be employing the strategies appropriate for that particular kind of hunting. What we find depends to a great extent on what we've looked for.

Social process: We usually think of reading as a solitary process, but in two ways, reading is a *social process*. It may seem too obvious to need to be stated, but reading is a *communicative* process in which the writer has reached out to the reader. But, the reader and writer are unknown to each other personally. Each has to imagine the intents and needs of the other, just as I am now writing this for you, but I don't know you, and you have no idea that I am writing this (for you) as I do so. But, there's communication between us right now nevertheless. We've found each other! If you think that your students don't need to be made aware of the writer-reader connection, if you think that they already understand that an actual person wrote their reading material, consider how they depersonalize the writer, referring to the writer as *they*. It may seem like a small point, but that use of the vague, nameless *they* reveals how disconnected the readers are from the human connection that is supposed to happen between writer and reader.

Cognitive process: Reading comprehension requires *all lights on* in the cognitive domain: mental representation, information, memory, language, attention. As a cognitive process, reading is not just decoding. It is decoding as a means of *coming to know*. We *come to know* when we add new information to existing information. Doing so is exactly what we mean by *cognitive process*.

Now, let's look at the part of the definition that talks about reading holistically.

Readers simultaneously use their knowledge of spoken and written language: Written language derives from speech, but it is not exactly the same. Written language has features, such as punctuation and paragraphing, that stand in for the pauses and inflections that spoken language has. The reader must learn to animate written language by turning on the mental reading voice. Deficit readers may not even know about the reading voice, without which they cannot connect text to human communication.

Knowledge of the topic of the text and their knowledge of their culture: The importance of prior knowledge about text and culture as a prerequisite to reading comprehension cannot be overstated. Here's an example from E. D. Hirsch, author of *The Knowledge Deficit* (Houghton Mifflin, 2006, quoted in *American Educator*, Spring 2006). The sentence "Jones sacrificed and knocked in a run," easily comprehensible to most Americans, would be far less comprehensible to a British reader. Hirsch explains that to comprehend this sentence, the reader would have to place it in the context of baseball, interpreting all of the key words (sacrificed, knocked in, run) in that context. If you didn't have the cultural capital about baseball, your ability to decode that sentence would not be sufficient to unlock its meaning. This is why building cultural capital, summoning prior knowledge, and being exposed to a variety of language experiences—formal and informal, academic and social—are essential for reading comprehension.

I think reading for comprehension is akin to the way threads engage fabric on a sewing machine: When you use a sewing machine, you have two threads, one upper and one lower. The two threads engage at the point of the fabric, and that's how machine sewing happens. But sometimes, the lower thread does not engage; maybe the bobbin is empty. You go along for several stitches, thinking that something useful is happening, only to realize that the upper thread has not been attaching to anything at all. The thread comes right up when you tug it slightly. It's just been looking and sounding like sewing has been happening. This non-sewing process reminds me of the non-reading of running one's eyes over text when the brain is in fact disengaged. The following key principles of reading comprehension explain more about engagement in text: what it means and how it happens.

Key Principles of Reading Comprehension

In this book, we're talking about reading comprehension, not decoding. By reading comprehension, we mean the ability to receive and process the writer's intended message: in other words, reading for communication between the reader and the absent writer.

Some students at the secondary level have not learned to decode. They can't translate the symbols on the page to make words. This inability can persist into secondary schooling for several reasons such as dyslexia, poor eyesight, and unfamiliarity with the alphabetic script and/or speech of the English language. This book does not address issues of neurology (dyslexia) or ophthalmology (poor eyesight), although students with these problems can certainly benefit from the research-based strategies to the extent that they need all the help they can get. I'm not going to say that this book addresses the needs of the Chinese or Arabic students who can read in the alphabet of their native languages, but who are English language learners. However, these students, too, need all the tools they can get their hands on, and so if you have such students (and who doesn't?) I hope you will remember that comprehension strategies can help *everyone*.

How can comprehension strategies help students who might not even notice if the book were held upside down? You will find that the strategies that I'm talking about are *thinking* strategies, helping students to concentrate and organize information into meaningful chunks. So, whereas your students with dyslexia, eye problems, and limited English proficiency still need specialized assistance, you can help them compensate.

We hear people say: "I read, but I don't understand what I read." This means: "I look like I'm reading, I call what I'm doing when my face is in the book reading, but I'm not reading." For the purpose of this book, and for all practical intents, reading *is* comprehension. Years ago, I decided to learn how to read Hebrew. I learned how to decode the text and make sounds, words, and sentences out of the squiggly lines, dots, and shapes. But, I didn't know what the words and sentences meant. Can we call that reading? *Yes,* in a way, but *no,* in a more significant way because I derived no significant meaning.

When we speak in this book of reading, what we mean is comprehension: meaning that is derived through the process of decoding printed messages. Meaning occurs when the reader says: "Okay, I recognize this information as something that I already knew," or "Okay, I recognize this as new information, and I know where it fits in that big puzzle in my brain that makes meaning out of the world." When new information acts like a puzzle piece that finds its place, that is *learning.* Our world has just gotten bigger; our world has just taken one more step toward making perfect sense to us.

But, there's a third possibility, and it looks like this: "Okay, I recognize this as new information, but I don't know what it means in terms of what I already know." You can hear Einstein's theory of relativity and understand every word, phrase, and sentence, but still not understand the sum of its parts. You might be able to parrot it, but it doesn't pass the preceding learning test because it hasn't made your world bigger or more sensible. It's just an unattached puzzle piece sitting on the side, a player on the bench whose value to the team you don't know. When you (think you've) *read* something, but you come away with either no recognizable information or no information that fits into your world, you have not comprehended.

There are internal and external reasons for noncomprehension. Internal reasons have to do with the emotional and physical conditions that the reader brings to the text.

The Reading Muse is a jealous mistress, demanding both stillness (of the body and of the environment, eliminating distracting stimuli) and activity (as the mind hears the voice and sees the images, and as the mind monitors comprehension and applies strategies to repair lapses). External reasons for noncomprehension have to do with what's in the text itself: the extent to which its content is unfamiliar and the extent to which it deals with abstract or symbolic concepts, sentence length and complexity, the percentage of unfamiliar and multisyllabic vocabulary. The difficulty—opaqueness, if you will—of text also has to do with other factors that load up the short-term memory: paragraph length, sentences that have a lot of intervening words between the subject and the verb, pronouns that refer to large amounts of text or that are separated from their referents by many words. Because there is so much that can stand between the reader's understanding and the writer's meaning, readers need to intervene, monitoring comprehension and then taking remedial action to repair lapses. Self-monitoring is a strategy that I will discuss in Chapter 2.

Fluency, the ability to read automatically, without having to break stride to implement basic processes such as decoding, is a crucial reader survival skill. Fluency comes from practice. Practice builds speed and stamina. This is why time set aside for sustained silent reading is valuable. It is entirely possible that the time that you give students to read is the only quiet time they have. Understand that in-class reading time is quality learning time. Don't hesitate to make it a regular part of your classroom routine, even if for only ten to fifteen minutes once a week. Imagine how much reading skills would improve if this were done throughout the school at different times during the student's week.

Strategy, Skill, Knowledge

Let's establish the difference between strategy, skill, and knowledge. A strategy is a way to build skills; skills lead to knowledge. If a reader can navigate through text that has unfamiliar words by figuring out their meaning either through word components or context clues (or both), doing so is a skill. If the reader can extract meaning through text that contains unfamiliar words *despite* those unfamiliar words, doing so is a skill. But if readers need to stop and think about what to do about unfamiliar words that are impeding meaning in text, and they make a conscious educated guess based on suffixes, roots, and prefixes, or based on what context clues tell them as they *reread* a sentence, doing so is a strategy. Once strategies become so internalized that they can be applied unconsciously, they can be considered skills. Skills can be improved through practice. Strategies must be explicitly taught, with the learner having explanations, modeling. guided practice, scaffolding, and reflection.

In old-fashioned education, the teacher paid little attention to strategy or skill, especially in the secondary grades. The so-called *chalk-and-talk* teacher operated on the dispenser of knowledge paradigm. He or she simply stood in front of the classroom talking and showing. The assumption was that the students would get it. Many did; many didn't. Many got it for the test, gave it back, and forgot it. Strategies for learning the skills that would make it possible to keep and use knowledge were not explicitly taught.

Constructivism is an educational philosophy and practice based on the belief that knowledge is constructed by the learner by integrating new information with existing knowledge. Information consists of just facts; knowledge consists of information plus the skills to use that information. Creativity cannot happen with information alone. Creativity results when we apply strategies and skills to knowledge to make new combinations.

Learning is not passive, as was once thought. Although part of learning is certainly the absorption of facts, students must have processing time. In a science class, processing time, traditionally, has been the *lab experience.* In foreign language classes, processing time is the time in which the students are speaking (later, writing) in the target language, preferably spontaneously and for real meaning. In English classes, processing time is the time when students are discussing or writing about what they've read. In social studies classes, processing time is the time when students are solving problems, debating issues, and creating models. And in math classes, processing time is the time when students are solving math problems.

The problem is that much processing time is relegated to the domain of homework, and homework is often not done. If done, it is done without the stimulation and learning cues of a classroom. We have to value processing time within the school day, and not just study hall.

We need to build processing time for reading, just as serious graduate students do when they form study groups. The difference is that your students aren't necessarily as motivated or as mature as graduate students who actively form study groups to help them process their reading, but the *need for process time is the same* whether you are a Harvard MBA student or a struggling student in a seventh grade social studies class. If the law school student needs processing time (talking, annotating, reviewing, diagramming), then we can see how our students not only need it, but need to learn strategies for information processing.

Cueing Systems

If you were an elementary school teacher, you'd be very used to hearing about the three *cueing systems,* as they are called, for reading (both decoding and comprehending). As a secondary teacher, you may not be familiar with this terminology, so I'll explain it because it's important in helping students on the secondary level as well.

The philosophy behind the notion of cueing systems is that the words, phrases, sentences, and whole text are *conspiring to tell you what they mean!* They are conspiring to do this by giving you the following hints (cues):

Graphophonic: That is, the word is spelled in a way that is conspiring to get you to associate it with other words that look like it. Or, the word has parts in it that you recognize. We use the word *graphophonic* because what we're talking about here is basic decoding, or, understanding the symbol-to-sound code. Graphophonic cues are hints that are given to you by the way a word arranges its letters in an arrangement that is familiar to you because you recognize it in other words.

Semantic: If you are a fluent speaker and listener in the language in which the text is written, you know what most of the words mean. Also, you know what the words mean in this particular context. There can be a few or more than a few words that you don't know, but the other words in the text are conspiring to help you make meaning even without knowing every word. Semantic cues are hints that are given to you by the words in the sentence which meaning you know.

Syntactic: Syntactic cues are cues that derive from the way in which the words come together to form phrases and sentences. Whether you think you know grammar or not, you do know it, and far more than you've been giving yourself credit for. You can distinguish the subject from the object (whether you know that you can or not); you can tell if the action is happening now, in the past, or in some hypothetical time zone; you can put words together in phrases. Syntactic cues are hints that the sentences are giving to you by marching the words in a certain order, conspiring to tell you what they mean in that order so that you recognize their relationship to each other.

But, I'm Not a Reading Teacher

You picked up this book because you want to improve student performance in reading for the subject that you specialize in. You have neither the time nor the training to address serious reading deficits, and yet the time you have been spending having to make up for the reading that students are not doing effectively is reducing the amount and depth that you can actually teach.

You say: "But, I'm not a reading teacher. I need to teach and assess my subject, not the student's reading development." I say: Your students' development in your subject is related to their development as *readers* in your subject. If you're not doing any reading teaching or assessment, how do you expect students to improve their ability to obtain, retain, and review information presented in your textbook?

You say: "But, I'm not a reading teacher. I want my professional development to be about my subject." I say: There's curriculum (your subject) and instruction (how you teach your subject). Professional development on a school-wide or district-wide basis is usually about the latter. For the former, you should attend conferences and read journals that specialize in your subject area. There, you will find the blend where instructional tools are embedded in your curriculum. But, don't be surprised if a lot of what you find there takes you right back into literacy issues because they are critical for student performance.

You say: "But, I'm not a reading teacher. It's all I can do to get through what I need to get through to prepare these kids for a state test." I say: If your students are poor readers, *you find yourself having to do the work for them* rather than having them able to make meaning for themselves. You could work more efficiently if you'd spend ten minutes a week on an organized series of mini-lessons that would enable your students to absorb information on their own, rather than having to explain and re-explain everything you need them to know for the state test.

You say: "But, I'm not a reading teacher. I know nothing about teaching phonics." I say: No one says you have to teach phonics or decoding skills. But you do teach terminology. Your students are learning a new language in your class. Teach words in clusters, as though a group of words on a related topic go together in a kit. Point out how complex words share similar components: prefix, root, suffix. When you have students using the glossary, don't just have them looks words up and write down definitions. Have them discover patterns, put words into categories, find relationships between words, create clusters of words that apply to a chapter.

What's the pay-off? Why should you bother? Research supports the assertion that the more your students read in your subject area, the smarter they will become in its language. The smarter they become in its language, the better they can understand its concepts. I hope to be able show you in this book how you can enhance student performance by including reading strategies as a part of your teaching.

2

Scaffolding Vocabulary Instruction

This book is about building comprehension of students, as a class, when they are faced with the requirement that they read large blocks of texts independently. This is not a book about how to teach dyslexic students how to decode, or how to address the needs of individual students who have serious deficits in letter-to-sound relationships. As content-area secondary school teachers, we can't address individual students who are best served by special programs such as the Wilson Reading Program or Orton-Gillingham. (These are phonic-based programs that are used for students whose grade-level peers are no longer in need of instruction in decoding.) What can we do for these students, then, and how can we help those students who do have noticeable deficits related to phonemic awareness and decoding?

One answer is to scaffold the reading task. Scaffolding is a learning support system of some kind that brings the students far enough along that they can complete the rest of task themselves. Scaffolding for reading instruction is not giving students the answers, doing the work for them, reading everything aloud for them, giving hints, or diluting the information and leaving it at that. None of those things empowers students to use the skills that they do have to learn what they need to learn. Scaffolding is providing enough cues to the reading to allow the student to extract meaning from the text.

One of the tenets of scaffolding is that sometimes it takes multiple exposures to something to understand it fully. The instructional implication is that some students need to have complex information or systems presented to them more than once and in more than one way. They may need a verbal explanation, *and* diagrams, *and* a hands-on experience *before they can understand the chapter*. In other words, they need a build-up of background knowledge before they can extract meaning from text. It's that build-up of background knowledge that we call scaffolding. Note that building up background knowledge is not *replacing* the reading requirement. It is simply boosting the student up to the point where the reading material is going to make sense. By the time the student reads the material, he or she has enough knowledge that he or she does not have to process the basics along with the details all once. That is the value of scaffolding.

Another related tenet of scaffolding is that we absorb only so much information at a time, and then we need to process it before we are ready to learn any more information. The instructional implication is the same as the preceding: We facilitate durable learning when we help students construct knowledge, brick by brick. If much of what we are asking them to read is new information, or, as in the case with novels, confusing information because the story contains mysteries, then we scaffold by breaking down the information into manageable pieces.

Finally, learning is a recursive process, not a linear one. What this means is that as we learn, we revisit previous experiences and add to them, just as when you return to a complex place, such as a city, you are able to notice and absorb more about it because you already have the basics down. We can use previous learning as a scaffold on which to base new information, but we sometimes need to be reminded to use what we already know to learn more.

It is extremely helpful to think about scaffolding when we teach students who can't access text either because of dyslexia, other learning disabilities such as attention-deficit/hyperactivity disorder (ADHD) or visual impairments, or because English is a foreign language to them.

The purpose of the following chart (see Figure 2.1) is to clarify what is and is not scaffolding in four different situations, and why.

Figure 2.1. Scaffolding

	Not Scaffolding	*Scaffolding*
Juliana is visually impaired.	Read aloud to Juliana. *This is not scaffolding because this is not giving Juliana the practice and adaptations that she will need in life to access text to the extent that she is able. We can't expect Juliana to do what is physically impossible for her, but we can do everything possible to make the text accessible to her limited eyesight.*	Provide large-print text. Seat Juliana close to the board. Use only black markers on a white board. Be mindful of Juliana's need to have large letters on the board.
Mitchell has ADHD	Tell Mitchell everything he needs to know, assuming that he won't read it. *This is not helping Mitchell manage his ADHD challenges. What he needs is to develop the routine of reading a certain amount, albeit small, and being accountable to make meaning of it.*	Break the reading expectations down into smaller units.

Chul Soo is an English-language learner (ELL).	Give Chul Soo the same reading and instruction as everyone else and hope for the best. Assume that his ELL teacher has everything under control. *No teacher in the English-speaking world should be without the skills to address the needs of our English language learners.*	Communicate with the ELL teacher. Have a Web site so that the ELL teacher can easily access your class activities. Provide word clusters of key words in the reading segment that Chul Soo is not likely to know from conversation. Learn all you can about the expected timelines for learning a new language. Offer extended time. Teach English word components.
Micah is dyslexic.	Eliminate the need for Micah to read. Provide other alternatives for him to get the information. *Dyslexia falls on a continuum. If a student is diagnosed as dyslexic that does not mean that he or she is incapable of reading anything at all. It means that he or she has difficulty to some extent. If we eliminate the need to read, then we guarantee that the dyslexic student will fall even further behind his or her peers.*	Provide cues such as pictures, word patterns, word clusters, graphic organizers. Work toward having Micah extract at least the main ideas from text. It's great to use visual cues for dyslexic students as long as those cues serve the reading, not replace it entirely. Offer extended time.
Anna has limited decoding skills.	Choose reading materials *for the entire class* that are at least two years below grade level so that Anna can read them. *Rather than lower the level of expectations to that of deficient readers, we need to provide sufficient support materials and instructions so that the deficient reader can access grade level text.*	Find controlled text (a simplified version of the text) to be used to establish sufficient background information that Anna can then access the remaining meaning from the authentic text. It would be better to have Anna read only parts of the grade level text than to excuse her from it entirely.

Gregory just never does any homework, is disengaged in class, and is failing multiple subjects in the ninth grade.	Assume that if Gregory continues to fail, he will eventually get the idea that he has to do some work to pass and will have learned a valuable life lesson. *Although Gregory does need to be held accountable, and although failure can certainly be a valuable lesson, we should not marginalize him any more than he is marginalizing himself. That is to say, we should not allow him to make an ostentatious display of inattention (such as putting his head down on his arms during class).*	Continue to make connections between the reading and the students interests and life. Continue to assume that Gregory will someday soon be available for academic learning. Continue to hold Gregory accountable for academic responsibilities and be optimistic about his chances for success despite his setbacks.

I believe strongly that the purpose of special education is to teach students adaptive strategies to the maximum extent possible rather than to excuse them from grade-level reading. Reading aloud to students should be used as a way for them to learn to improve their own reading skills, not as the primary way in which they receive information from text. Whenever we engage in alternative ways for students to gain information, we need to ask ourselves, "Is this alternative to reading going to result in the student's ability to be a better reader?" In other words, "Am I teaching the student a strategy for making meaning out of text," or "Am I enabling this student to continue life as a functional nonreader?" I maintain that to do the latter in the interest of what we think is efficiency is not helpful. And, I maintain that we can do the former to the benefit of all students, not just those with special needs.

Word Recognition at the Secondary Level

As I've said, students who haven't mastered basic sight vocabulary or the basics of the sound-symbol decoding system of reading are in need of specialized remediation. Let's realize, though, that, needful as such students are, they are a small minority. There's a much larger number of students who do have the basics but have deficits in the kinds of word recognition skills that are necessary to read academic text. To put it bluntly, these students need to learn how to read big words. Their inability to decode polysyllabic words impedes their fluency, and lack of fluency impedes comprehension significantly.

Therefore, to make students fluent readers of academic text at the secondary level, we need to teach them Latin and Greek word components. Words with Latin and Greek word components comprise the bulk of polysyllabic words in academic text. Because these words may not be encountered anywhere *except* in text and in academic conversation, they warrant specific attention.

We are looking at two kinds of word components: affixes (prefixes and suffixes) and stems (also known as roots). We can think of these as a word-making kit for academic language.

The stems or roots determine the essential meaning of the word. The way the English language works is that a Latin stem produces a word tree whose leaves, as it were, are all related. It's easier to detect some word-to-stem relationships than others. The stem itself has morphed a bit over time. For example, the stem *miss*- meaning *to send* can appear as *miss*- (remission, commission, emission, omission), or *mit*- (remit, commit, emit, omit). The stem *pos*- meaning to *put or place* as in *position, depose, impose,* can appear as *pon*- (component, exponent).

The English language has hundreds of Latin word stems from which we derive thousands of words. Figure 2.2 presents a partial list of some of the most accessible and useful ones for students:

Figure 2.2. Latin Word Stems

cede, ceed, cess: *to go, to yield*	accede, access concede, concession exceed, excessive necessary, necessitate process, procession recede, recession secession, succession
clud, clus, clos: *to close*	clause, cloister, closet, conclude, conclusion enclose, exclude, exclusion include, inclusion occlude, occlusion preclude, preclusion recluse, reclusive seclude, seclusion
cur, curs; *to run*	current, currency, cursive, cursor, cursory discursive incur, incursion occur, occurrence recur, recursive, recurrent

duct, duce: *to lead, to pull*	abduct, abductor, abduction, aqueduct conduct duct, ductile deduce, deduct, deduction induce, induct, inducement, induction produce, product, producer, productive reduce, reductive seduce, seduction, seductive transducer
fac, fic: *to do, to make*	de facto faction fact, factor factory fiction, fictitious manufacture
fer, phor: *to carry*	confer, conference, conifer defer, deference, deferential differ, difference, different, differential, differentiate infer, inference, inferential metaphor, metaphorical offer phosphorescence refer, reference, referent suffer, sufferance, insufferable transfer, transference
flec, flex: *to bend*	deflect, deflection flexible, flexibility genuflect, genuflection inflect, inflection reflect, reflection
flu, flux: *flow*	affluence, affluent confluence effluent flue, fluent, fluency influence, influx reflux, suffuse, superfluous

gress, grad: *to step*	aggression, aggressive congress, congressional degrade egress grade, gradient graduate ingress progress, progressive, progression regress, regressive, regression retrograde
ject: *to throw*	adjective abject deject, dejection inject, injection object, objective, objectify subject, subjective trajectory
lat: *side*	lateral, bilateral, unilateral latitude relate, relative, relationship
mit, miss: *to send*	admit, permit, remit, emit, omit, transmit, admission, permission, remission, emission, omission, transmission, mission, missionary, submit, submissive, submission
morph: *shape*	morpheme, morphology, amorphous, polymorphous, ectomorph, mesomorph, endomorph, metamorphosis
mot: *to move*	motility, motivate, motive, remote, demote, promote
nom, nym: *to name*	nominate, denominator, nominal, ignominy, nomenclature, synonym, acronym, homonym

pel, pul: *to drive*	impel, propel, repel, dispel, expel, compel, impulse, propeller, propulsion, repulsive, expulsion, compulsion
plic, plex: *to fold*	complicate, complicit, implicate, explicate, explicit, implicit accomplice, supplicate, duplicate, replicate complex
port: *to carry*	transport, import, export, portable, deport, report, support, port, opportunity
pos, pon: *to put or place*	position, depose, deposition, disposition, repose, suppose, expose, exposure, exposition, expository, impose, imposition
reg, rect: *straight*	rectangle, regular, rectify, erect, rectitude, correct, direct
script, scribe: *write*	transcript, scripture, conscription, prescription, subscription, prescribe, transcribe, subscribe, proscribe, inscribe, inscription, describe, description, manuscript
sect, sec: *to cut*	section, secular, bisect, dissect, intersect, transect, sector, secant
ten, tin, tain, tang, tex, tec, tac, teg: *to touch, to hold*	ascertain, attack, attain, attend, attention contain, containment, contend, contention, contingent, contingency detain, detention, detainee extend, extensive, extension integer, integral, integrity, intact, intend, intensive, intention maintain, maintenance pretend, pretense, pretension, pretext retain, retention sustain, sustenance tactile, tacky, tact, texture, tenure, tenant, tenet, texture, text, tangential

tract: *to drag, to draw*	attract, attractive, attraction contract, contraction detract distract, distraction extract, extraction intractable protract, protractor, protracted retract, retraction subtract, subtraction traction, tractor, tractable
veh, vect: *to carry*	convection vector, vehicle
vert, vers: *to turn*	averse, aversion, avert, adversity converse, controversy, convert, conversion diverse, diversion, divert inverse, inversion obverse reverse, reversion, revert subvert, subversive, subversion versatile, verse

The preceding stems usually appear in the middle of the word. Figure 2.3 presents a few more that usually appear at the beginning of words. Yet, they can't be considered prefixes because they are an integral part of the word. (A prefix would have to be removable from the word, leaving the word intact, such as *reread* or *preview.*

Figure 2.3. Latin Word Stems That Occur at the Beginning of the Word

ambi, amphi	ambivalent, ambidextrous, amphibian, amphibious,
dyna: *power*	dynamic, dynamo, dynasty
per: *through*	permeate, permeable, perspire, perforate, persuade
bene: *good*	benefit, note bene, benefactor, benevolent, beneficiary, benign
mal: *bad*	malnutrition, malcontent, malefactor, malice, malicious, malignant
meta: *beyond, change*	metamorphosis, metacognition, metaphysical, metaphor, metabolism
mut: *change*	mutable, mutation, immutable, mutiny
syn: *together*	synthesis, synchronize, syntax, synergy
con, com: *together*	convene, compress, contemporary, converge, compact, conduct, confluence, committee, communal, constituent, component
trans: *across*	transcontinental, transient, transdermal, transitory, transition, transit, transport, transfer
equi: *balance*	equal, equilateral, equidistant, equilibrium

The prefixes in Figure 2.4 indicate spatial relationships and are frequently found in academic language.

Figure 2.4. Spatial Relationship Prefixes

ecto, exo: *outside*	exoskeleton
extra: *in addition*	extrapolate, extraterrestrial
inter: *between*	interaction, interactive, intercoastal, interpersonal
peri: *around*	perimeter, periscope, perinatal
super, supra: *beyond*	supernova, superfluous

When you present the roots, always be sure to have at least one familiar word in the list of derivatives, so that the student can connect new information to known information. If all of the derivatives are new words, the student will just think, "Here are a bunch of words that I don't know."

And, note that teaching word components has the added benefit of teaching spelling clusters as well. Students become better spellers when they see clusters, rather than thinking that English words are spelled at random.

In addition, we have many words that populate academic text with Latin or Greek origins expressed at the ends of words (but not as suffixes). These words are particularly common in mathematics and science, and they are also common in social studies. Figure 2.5 shows these words.

Figure 2.5. Latin and Greek Stems That Occur at the Ends of Words

-us	apparatus, bacillus/bacilli, locus/loci, focus/foci, fungus/fungi, radius/radii, sinus stimulus/stimuli, syllabus/syllabi, terminus, virus
-um, as the singular -a, as the plural	bacterium/bacteria, datum/data, medium, media; referendum, referenda
-ex, -ix	apex, appendix/appendices; index/indeces/ matrix/matrices/vortex/vortices
-is	analysis, epiglottis, glottis, metropolis, synopsis
-on	criterion/criteria, electron, horizon, neutron, phenomenon, polyhedron, tetrahedron

Common Phonemic Blends in Greek-Based Words

The Greek-based words are extremely important in academic understanding, and the way that they are spelled can be off-putting to inexperienced readers. Certain letter clusters typify Greek-based words, and special attention should be paid to them because of their usefulness and possible unfamiliarity to deficient readers:

♦ Ph: Words that have the *ph* combination having the sound of *f* are always Greek-based and deserving to special attention, such as: phonics, phonetic, alphabet, physical, physics, graphic, photosynthesis geography, and so on.

♦ —y: When a word has a *y* as its second letter, that word is Greek-based and deserves special attention: mystery, dynamics, cycle, gyrate, hypothesis, lyrics, symmetry, tyrant, and so forth.

♦ Ch: Used in such words as psychology, chaos, chemical, chroma, chromosome.

♦ Sci: Found in science, conscience, conscientious.

Other words of Greek origin that deserve special attention are words that end in -ology, *words with the unvoiced th- sound (theme, thesis), words ending in -sis (crisis, thesis, synthesis), those having a the kn- or -gn- that have to do with knowledge: (knowledge, acknowledge, agnostic).*

Principles of Vocabulary Learning

♦ We learn words through multiple exposures. Each exposure to a word in context gives us a bit more information about the word's meaning and forms.

♦ Learning a new word, or understanding the components of a familiar one, brings opportunities to learn other words in clusters. The clusters can be component-related, such as the preceding word-stem clusters , or they can be grammatical, as in the following morphology chart (Figure 2.6).

Figure 2.6. Target Word Morphology Chart

Target words: Synthesis (noun), Product (noun), Obscure (adjective), Comply (verb)

Noun	Verb	Adjective	Adverb
Synthesis	Synthesize	Synthetic	Synthetically
Product Productivity Production	Produce	Productive	Productively
Obscurity	Obscure	Obscure	Obscurely
Compliance	Comply	Compliant	Compliantly

We can also learn words in clusters of similar meaning, or words that might be used to discuss a particular subject, establishing word banks that enable the novice to enter the conversation like a professional.

♦ Because we learn words through multiple exposures, we need to elevate our language when we speak to students, defining words casually, within our own sentences as we speak. Thus, the skilled teacher develops a kind of layered speech, using terms that can be unfamiliar to some listeners, compensating by defining the terms casually in the course of communication.

♦ The difference between close words is established as in the following list.

• Foundation, premise, basis, theme

- Civilization, culture

- Belief, religion, tenet, faith

- Hypothesis, theory, guess, thesis

◆ Deep understandings of a few central words will prepare the mind for functional understandings of peripheral words. By deep understandings, I mean the following:

- Recognition of word components

- Identification of words with similar components

- Etymology (history and development of the word through the ages)

- Nuance and connotation, if applicable (emotional associations with that word)

- Cross-disciplinary use

A teacher whose chief vocabulary-building tool is having students look words up in a dictionary is building vocabulary one word at a time, and that is assuming that the student will actually remember the word looked up, let alone use it, let alone use it in its proper context and in its full scope. But the teacher who thoroughly *explains* a word and then uses that word as the key to unlocking meanings of related words builds vocabulary much faster and with more likelihood of durable learning.

Academic Language Toolbox

We've been talking about polysyllabic words, and, important as they are in academic reading, I'd like to set aside space for one- and two-syllable words that are the nuts and bolts of academic reading and which, because they are so unassuming, can be overlooked. (See Figure 2.7) These words are crucial for our English language learners and our students with learning disabilities pertaining to language. This list is gleaned from an *Building Academic Vocabulary* by Lawrence Zwier (2002). I think it's important to pay attention to these words because—think about it—if your students get to secondary school without immediate comprehension of these basic words, they'd surely be lost in what you're expecting them to read.

You'll note, as you run through the lists, the versatility of these words, how they not only are used throughout the school day, but how they take on different meanings from class to class. You can have students, especially English language learners, who don't have the flexibility to adapt a word from one genre to another, which would be a major impediment to comprehension.

Figure 2.7. Language Toolboxes

Toolbox 1: One-Syllable Words Essential for Reading Comprehension			
Aid	File	Phase	Solve
Add	Form	Place	State
Brief	Frame	Plan	Sum
Chart	Goal	Plot	Task
Claim	Graph	Plus	Term
Class	Hence	Point	Test
Code	Key	Prove	Theme
Clue	List	Rank	Trace
Draft	Mean	Rare	Trait
Fact	Note	Root	Via
Fee	Pace	Rule	

Toolbox 2: Two-Syllable Words Essential for Reading Comprehension			
Abstract	Conduct	Domain	Format
Access	Conflict	Data	Founded
Achieve	Credit	Define	Guidelines
Adult	Consent	Derive	Extract
Affect	Constant	Design	Global
Alter	Contact	Debate	Gender
Approach	Civil	Despite	Granted
Area	Cycle	Decline	Highlight
Aspect	Cited	Diverse	Income
Assume	Channel	Export	Involve
Attain	Comprise	Ensure	Issues
Author	Compose	Exclude	Impact
Aware	Convert	Emerge	Item
Behalf	Couple	Error	Imply
Bias	Crucial	Ethnic	Impose
Concept	Device	Enhance	Image
Context	Devote	Estate	Ignore
Contract	Denote	Factor	Index
Control	Detect	Function	Journal
Create	Displace	Final	Labor
Chapter	Deny	Focus	Legal
Complex	Decade	Framework	Locate
Compound	Dispose	Finite	License

Logic	Offset	Rely	Thereby
Lecture	Process	React	Topic
Mature	Progress	Region	Transmit
Mental	Purchase	Research	Series
Input	Publish	Respond	Status
Insert	Predict	Require	Thesis
Induce	Prior	Release	Theory
Intense	Pursue	Reverse	Transfer
Minor	Passive	Reject	Technique
Major	Portion	Section	Target
Method	Prospect	Sector	Transport
Maintain	Refine	Segment	Transform
Normal	Relax	Structure	Volume
Negate	Restrain	Select	Version
Notion	Rigid	Survey	Vision
Neutral	Random	Sequence	Visual
Overseas	Restore	Style	Unique
Option	Revise	Symbol	Unit
Output	Review	Survive	Whereas
Outcome	Regime	Somewhat	Whereby
Obtain	Retain	Solely	Widespread
Occur	Remove	Trigger	

Summary

Chapter 2 has been about building the foundations of knowledge about words, making it possible for students to extract meaning from text. When we get to the bottom of what students know, we can use what they *already know* to learn what they *need to know.* That is what scaffolding is all about.

Vocabulary learning is always about scaffolding. We can already know something about a word because we know other words having common parts. We can already know something about a word because we understand nearby parts of the text that it is in. However, if a student doesn't have basic understandings, such as knowing the words in the preceding toolboxes, then we have to go there *first* because the student who lacks basic knowledge about how the English language is used *academically* cannot access the sophisticated information contained in secondary school reading.

3

Standardized Tests and Reading Comprehension

We cannot overlook the importance of student performance on reading comprehension questions that appear, directly or indirectly, on standardized tests.

In Chapter 3, we'll take a look at the kinds of reading that students need to do for standardized tests, and how strategic reading lessons embedded in the content area curriculum can address them.

In a sense, all multiple choice, true/false, fill-in-the-blank, and matching column questions, short constructed response, and essay tests are reading comprehension questions because the test-taker has to read the questions and items well enough to supply the correct answer. But let's take a close look at the pure reading comprehension tests, those that present a passage to be read followed by questions that theoretically can't be answered through prior knowledge alone but whose answers depend solely on comprehension of the given passage.

Certainly, these are high-stakes tests. Results can determine a student's placement and eligibility for remediation, or, on the other side of the spectrum, advancement. SATs and similar gate-keeping tests, including graduate-level admissions tests, have a reading comprehension component. State exams that determine a school's reputation in the public eye to a large extent have a reading comprehension component. So, by any measure, these tests are important enough for me to state that the strategies that we use to improve reading academic texts should also improve performance on standardized reading comprehension tests.

Do reading comprehension test questions address the same kind of meaning-making that we've been discussing throughout this book? They do, but that doesn't mean that you should teach to a reading comprehension test instead of embedding strategy-based instruction into content area lessons. If you teach to the test, the skills will not carry over to everyday reading, but if you consistently and systematically teach strategies for everyday reading, research indicates that those skills will carry over into the testing situation if you also prepare students for the test format.

Preparing for a test and teaching to a test are not the same things. Preparing for a test means giving students practice in the test format so that they can get used to timing themselves and not have the anxiety of seeing a test format for the first time when they actually sit down to take the text. It's important that test-takers know what the test looks like and how long it will take them to answer the questions.

Reading comprehension test questions tend to fall into six categories. There's no reason why we shouldn't familiarize ourselves with these question categories and include them in our strategic mini-lessons, as all of them do fit into our strategies.

Main idea questions: These are sometimes phrased as "Which of the following would be the best title for this passage?" or "The author's most important point in this passage is…" As part of our strategy of using textual features and other cues to determine what is most important in text, we can have students compose titles and explicitly identify main ideas in text to prepare them for this question category.

The vocabulary in context question: Usually, the question wants to know if the reader is flexible enough to relinquish a traditional definition of a word for one that suits an unusual context, especially where the word in question has a metaphorical meaning. For example, note the words in the following sentence that use personifying metaphors to convey the sound of the wind through the trees in this sentence: *You can hear the wind, in the sighing pines, the whistling skitter of the crisp leaves, the swirling leaves in the gust, still restless, not yet settled into their winter bed.* The test-taker would be expected to recognize that the word *sighing* is not literal but a metaphorical way of getting the reader to hear the whoosh of wind through the autumn leaves.

We can prepare students for the vocabulary in context question by encouraging them to slow down when they read descriptive text and by weighing the words, that is: *Why this word instead of another that has a similar meaning? What is the author trying to make me visualize and feel with a particular word?*

The author's intent question: These questions want to know if the reader perceives connotation based on word choice. For example, the following sentences have several words that reveal the author's attitude about winter: *Highways are blocked, power lines crippled, communities isolated. We live beleaguered under the threat of winter's wind.*

Like the vocabulary in context question, the author's intent question is asking for readers to pick up on the subtleties of words and images. Prior knowledge comes into play as readers agree to go along with how the author uses particular word choices to convey not only information but emotions and attitude about the information.

The internal organization question: This is a question that wants to know if the test-taker notices the road signs of narrative, description, classification, definition, exemplification, cause and effect, comparison/contrast, or process analysis (sequence). If students have learned the *during reading* strategy of recognizing text pattern clusters, they are ready for this kind of question.

The drawing conclusions question: This question combines the thinking of the main idea question with that of the author's intent question. The question wants to know if the reader has understood it well enough to carry through on the writer's thoughts. The invisible word for drawing conclusions is *therefore*. If students have extensive training in reading for cause and effect, they should be prepared to answer reading comprehension questions that call for drawing conclusions.

The part-to-whole question: This is a question that wants to know if the test-taker can analyze the text. How is a detail related to the main idea? Why is a particular anecdote given? Why does the piece begin and end the way it does? What is the relationship between a sentence and the one that follows it? If students have been expressing meaning through graphic organizers that show the relationship between main and supporting ideas, they should be prepared to answer the part-to-whole question.

What follows are some sample reading comprehension questions representing an array of the types of the preceding questions.

Example: Reading Comprehension Test

Note that the sentences are numbered, so that we can refer to them easily.

(1) Modern Caribbean culture is rich with the history of its cultural mixing. (2) The Afro-Caribbean roots of the thirteen island-nations that comprise the Caribbean region are reflected in their music, food, and traditions. (3) Music such as calypso, reggae, and salsa pulse through the minds and hearts of the more than thirty million people of the Caribbean islands. (4) If you visit these beautiful shores, you'll hear Spanish, English, Dutch, and French. (5) These were the languages of the people who brought the Africans as slaves to the islands. (6) But you'll also hear Creole, a language that was created from the African tongues mixed with the European language of the slavers who were in power. (7) You'll taste the sweet and spicy flavors of fufu, fried plantains, curried goat, and cassava pone. (8) The Caribbean people take pride in their lifestyles. (*continues on page 34*)

(9) After slavery ended in the latter half of the nineteenth century, the former slaves reclaimed their African heritage as much as they could. (10) The beginning of the twentieth century established many of the island-nations as independent entities, most of which are now flourishing democracies where the people value their African heritage.

Main Idea Question

Which of the following statements best expresses the main idea of this passage:

1. The road to independence in the Caribbean was difficult and violent.
2. The people of the Caribbean island-nations speak many languages.
3. Modern Caribbean nations reflect their African heritage along with the influences of the enslavers of the Africans brought there.
4. The economy of the Caribbean islands was based on the institution of slavery.

Analysis

The correct answer is (3). The first choice is incorrect because the passage does not stress the difficulty and violence of the road to Caribbean independence, although the statement itself may be true. Choice (2) is incorrect because the statement, although true, represents a detail and not an idea that infuses every sentence, which the main idea would have to do. Choice (4), although a true statement, is incorrect because it makes a point that is not developed in the passage. A good clue to the correctness of choice (3) is the lead sentence of the passage, which, in this case, does encapsulate the main idea. The first and last sentences of reading passages are likely places to find the main idea. In this case, looking in the likely places does give us the correct response.

Vocabulary in Context Question

In sentence (10), the word entities means the same or nearly the same as which of the following words or phrases in the passage:

1. regions
2. island-nations
3. democracies
4. heritage

Analysis

The correct response is (2) because the sentence implies that the unit that is being called an *entity* is a finite governmental state, rather than a *region* (1). It could be an independent entity without necessarily being a democracy (3). Choice (4), *heritage,* does not fit grammatically into the sentence because it is not plural. Also, there's no such thing as an independent heritage because the word *independent* refers to politics and economics whereas *heritage* refers to culture and lifestyle.

Author's Intent Question

The reader can assume that the author's attitude toward Afro-Caribbean culture is
1. positive.
2. negative.
3. both positive and negative.
4. neither positive nor negative.

Analysis

Words with positive connotations such as *modern* and *rich* set the positive tone of the author's attitude toward the subject, the Afro-Caribbean people and their land and culture. Although the references to enslavers are clearly negative, the passage is more about the triumph and cultural reclamation of the African people than about their enslavement. Therefore, the author's attitude is overwhelmingly positive, and the only sensible choice is (1).

Internal Organization Question

This passage is developed primarily through
1. comparison/contrast.
2. example.
3. definition.
4. narrative.

Analysis

Once we know that the main idea is encapsulated in the first sentence, we can see that the piece is developed primarily through examples (2) that illustrate the claim that "Modern Caribbean culture is rich with the heritage of its cultural mixing." Although two groups, the enslavers and the Africans, are mentioned, they are not being compared, so choice (1) is incorrect. The piece does not set forth a definition (3), nor does it present a narrative (4) because there's no main character.

Drawing Conclusions Question

Which of the following statements can the reader most clearly infer from the passage:
1. The author has recently returned from a vacation to a Caribbean island.
2. The author is of Afro-Caribbean descent.
3. The author predicts instability in the Caribbean region.
4. The author thinks that democracy is a good form of government.

Analysis

Although the author is obviously enthusiastic about the Caribbean island-nations and would probably enjoy a vacation there, there's no reason to assume that either choice (1) or (2) are correct. As for choice (3), although instability is certainly common when several cultures converge on the same piece of land, there is no implication in this passage that instability is present. The word *flourishing* to describe democracy in the last sentence, along with the consistently positive tone of the passage, would lead us to the conclusion that (4) is the correct response.

Part-to-Whole Question

Sentence (6) begins with the word *But* because of which of the following:
1. Creole is a more widely spoken language than the European languages.
2. The author wants the reader to know that the European languages are not the only ones spoken in the Caribbean island-nations.
3. The author wants the reader to know that not all of the African languages that were brought to the Caribbean disappeared.
4. Creole is a kind of language that results from cultural mixing when people of different languages must communicate, usually to do business.

Analysis

If you didn't read all of the choices, you might have settled for (2), which is a valid response but not the best one given. Choice (3) is the better response because it more accurately captures the author's main idea that important strains of African culture, including language, have survived in the Caribbean. Choice (1) has no evidence to substantiate it; choice (4) is a correct definition of a Creole language, but it does not respond to the question.

Example: Science Tests

Look over the following sample science test question.

---

1. A river whose water is used as the chief water supply for a city has had its mercury levels measured for a period of 10 years. The measurements are represented in the following graph:

   Water is considered unsafe if its mercury levels rise above 5×10 grams of mercury per liter (g/L). What inference would you draw from the preceding graph?
   a.   The water has been unsafe since these measurements were taken.
   b.   The water will become unsafe within 5 years.
   c.   The water will continue to be safe for at least 10 years.
   d.   The graph does not indicate the safety of the water.

2. Which of the following phenomena best represents a cyclical event?
   a.   The yearly rate at which a glacier melts
   b.   Sonar measurements of oceanic depth
   c.   The variation of snowfall predictions
   d.   The appearance of star constellations at various points in the year

3. The phases of the moon are examples of
   a.   noncyclic events.
   b.   unrelated events.
   c.   predictable changes.
   d.   random motion.

Science

Why a Student Might Have Difficulty Comprehending This Text

Students need to bring the same metacognitive processes to a reading comprehension test as they do to other kinds of reading. That is, they need to reread, visualize, activate prior knowledge, attend to textual patterns, and use context clues to access unfamiliar vocabulary. The difference, of course, is that the information in the choices themselves cannot be trusted. The reader has to process the information in each choice, mentally fit it into the sentence or match it to the question, and then judge not only if it is correct or incorrect, but if it is better than the other choices presented.

Although we like to believe that multiple choice questions such as the preceding ones are testing for science information, they are testing just as mightily for *reading comprehension in the field of science*. Think about it: The student learns the information through listening to a lecture, watching a demonstration, doing a laboratory experiment and writing about it, talking about the information with a lab partner, *and* reading the textbook. But, the assessment cues the student only through reading comprehension. The validity of the test rests on the assumption that reading comprehension—specifically, the kind of reading comprehension that one needs for a multiple choice question—is a given skill. But, is it? Have we included the skill of reading multiple choice questions in our instruction? Or is it a skill that appears *only* in assessment? When we look at it this way, we see that lack of strategic reading instruction in domain-specific multiple choice test questions can itself be the impediment to success.

Multiple choice questions such as the preceding ones have their *own* vocabulary and sentence style, apart from the knowledge that is supposedly being tested. In question 1, the test-taker is expected to know what the word *inference* means. I'm wondering how often the teacher uses phrases such as "what inference would you draw from…" I know that a science teacher is not a reading teacher, but wouldn't any teacher whose students take multiple choice tests need to have awareness that the language of these tests needs to be taught, as well as the concepts?

Here is a sampling of the kind of phraseology that is found on a formal science assessment for ninth-grade students:

- Which of these statements is most likely an inference?

- What is the best inference that can be made from this data?

- Which statement best illustrates a…?

- Which statement best represents…?

- Which of the following best describes a…?

- Which graph best represents the relationship between ____and ____?

- Which statement best explains the observation?

- Which statement about ____is most accurate?

Now let's consider the sentence styles often found in multiple choice test items. Not all of the test items are questions, syntactically. Many are broken statements, where the test-taker is required to complete the sentence, often by supplying a direct object, as in the following:

To obtain the data recorded in the preceding graph, the technician used…

Sometimes, the object of a preposition must be supplied, such as in the following partial statement:

Remains of sea shells, plant life, and animal bones are likely to be found in…

Rarely is the test-taker asked to find the subject of the sentence; rarely, the verb. The instructional implication is that to improve reading comprehension on multiple choice tests, we need to have a close look at the vocabulary and sentence styles of the questions, and we need to familiarize test-takers with that kind of language. We can familiarize them with test-taking language in at least five ways:

1. Make it a habit to use the kind of language (vocabulary and sentence styles) that the test uses in the course of your explanations and directions.

2. Encourage students to write their own test items, using similar word choice.

3. Give abundant test samples, and have students compose an inventory of high frequency phrases.

4. Give special attention to complex sentence styles, such as the *if/then* formation, *toward which, with which, in the direction of,* and so forth.

5. Give students the first few words of a question. Have them predict how that question is going to develop.

In other words, treat the test language itself as content. Remember that every subject area does have domain-specific language that is not going to be taught in English class, where students are going to be spending most of their time reading literary text. Make connections between the common vocabulary from one subject to another, but "adjust the temperature of the words" as they are used in your subject.

Let's look at the following science test question:

III. The focal depth pattern shown on the cross section represents the location of the subsurface boundary between the two tectonic plates. Describe the relative motion of the plates along this boundary.

Why a Student Might Have Difficulty Comprehending This Text

I almost don't know where to begin to unpack the challenges that a struggling reader might have on the preceding test item. Let's begin with the fact that the student is being asked to comprehend this very dense text but to examine and comprehend a diagram at the same time.

As to vocabulary, we have the individual words *focal, subsurface,* and *tectonic* as the most obvious trouble-makers. Of these, only the last is truly unfamiliar. The student can use word component skills to access *focal* from *focus, subsurface* from *surface* and *sub.* But, accessing individual words is not the vocabulary problem in this sentence: The vocabulary problem lies in the phrases, where the meaning is more than the sum of the parts: *focal depth pattern, cross section, subsurface boundary, relative motion.* Such phrases need to be taught as if they were single words. Fortunately, except for *relative motion,* the phrases represent concrete images (rather than abstract concepts), and the student should be reminded to visualize them when reading.

Now, let's see what kind mischief the sentence style has created. Sentences are most comprehensible when the subject is a person; the subject is short; and the simple subject is right next to the verb. None of those three conditions is present in this sentence. The whole subject, *The focal depth pattern shown on the cross section*, is a lot more complex than a subject having just one concrete or proper noun with an adjective or two modifying it. This subject has three nouns (depth, pattern, section), all of which are somewhat abstract in that they don't bring to mind an immediate specific image for the reader. That is to say, the reader does not have stored reference for the subject. She has to create a brand new reference by looking at the diagram, a new image. And, the subject has within it a passive verb construction, *shown*. When presented with a complex, abstract subject such as this, the reader can use the strategy of shrink-wrapping the subject with the word *it*. The word *it* will encapsulate any noun phrase or noun clause. That little trick can make the sentence easier to handle.

Represents is the verb and although considered an action verb, there's not really any action, thus rendering the sentence even more abstract.

The third slot of the sentence, the direct object of the verb *represents*, comprises the rest of the sentence, and you can see that it is quite long and has two prepositional phrases. So, there's a lot of noun processing in this sentence without a strong action verb to help you see how the subject is affecting the direct object. And all this is on a *science* test.

What to do? The strategic reader can learn how to handle a sentence such as this analytically, short-cutting the sentence into its essential components:

The pattern represents the boundary.

That is the core (subject-verb-object) of this sentence, and the other words are modifiers. Grammatically, this is actually considered a simple sentence because it has just one clause. But, that clause has a lot of modification, preceding and following the key nouns that can cause the reader to be perplexed. The reader who knows how to strip the sentence down to its bare bones is at an advantage. I know you're not a reading teacher, you may be a science teacher and not an English teacher, or an English teacher and not a science teacher, but I want you to see that what's happening is that no one is teaching this test-taker to do what I just did and access meaning from a sentence such as this.

And, this sentence isn't even the question. This is just the introduction to the question. How can the test-taker even begin to select the right answer when the *introduction* to the question defeats her because of its wording?

What will be necessary here will be careful rereading and matching the nouns in the sentence to their correspondents in the diagram.

The best way to prepare students for a reading comprehension test is to have them construct questions for each of the major question types, explaining the correct and incorrect answers, as I've just done. To write good multiple choice questions, you have to know something about how to frame the distracters (wrong answers). Novices might present distracters that are so obviously wrong that the question loses its challenge. The distracters have to be either true statements that don't respond to the question, or true statements that are not addressed by the passage, or responses that are too broad or too narrow to answer the question satisfactorily.

A common trap in multiple choice questions is to go for an answer that is valid but not the best response of the four because the correct response is more accurate, more encompassing, or more specific. The test-maker and test-taker have to keep in mind that we're not looking just for statements that happen to be true: We're looking for statements that are true *and* that answer the question more thoroughly than the other choices *and* that are knowable because of the information in the reading passage. Writing good multiple choice questions and choices is a sophisticated skill and one worth cultivating as means of preparing for the questions written by professionals. It's intelligent, rather than rote, test preparation.

II

Academic Genres

4

Academic Genres: Subject Area Reading

It used to be thought that "reading is reading." That is, if you can read one kind of text, you can read anything. Thus, this was the way that most reading, both decoding and comprehension, was taught was during the time designated for English Language Arts in elementary schools. Most of the reading that students cut their teeth on was story text. It was assumed that they could transfer what they learned about comprehending and retaining story text to informational text. Now we know more about how reading comprehension and retention actually works: We understand much more about the domain-specific nature of reading skills, and how they don't so easily walk themselves over from the room in which story text is taught to the rooms in which other kinds of subjects are taught.

What follows is an explanation of how reading expectations differ from class to class.

What Kind of Reading Is Expected in Math Class?

About Math Language

Math language is very domain-specific. That is to say, math language constitutes its very own genre. I'll define genre as a defined territory of language that uses specialized language and favors certain kinds of sentence structure.

One of the reasons for math language being its very own genre is that its terminology cannot be figured out through context. The reader needs to know the mathematical definitions *before* reading them in the context of a mathematical explanation, procedure, or problem. For this reason, a lot of reading in math is the reading of definitions.

One of the favored kinds of sentence structure for math writers is what the grammarians call *passive voice structure.* In passive voice structure, the agent of the action is hidden. The opposite of passive voice structure is *active voice structure*, in which the agent of the action is placed as the subject of the sentence, with the result

45

being a clear sequence about who (or what) is doing what to whom (or what). The following examples will clarify the difference between passive and active voice constructions (see Figures 4.1 and 4.2).

Figure 4.1. Ordinary English Sentence Structure

Passive Voice Construction	*Active Voice Construction*
The ball was thrown.	The pitcher threw the ball.
The volume was adjusted.	I adjusted the volume.
The problem was solved.	We solved the problem.

Figure 4.2. Mathematical English Sentence Structure

Passive Voice Construction	*Active Voice Construction*
A number that can be written as a fraction with an integer numerator and a nonzero integer denominator is called a rational number.	If you can write a number as a fraction with an integer numerator and a nonzero integer denominator, then you can call it a rational number.
To subtract a polynomial from another polynomial, the opposite of each term of the polynomial that is being subtracted is added.	To subtract a polynomial from another polynomial, you need to add the opposite of each term of the polynomial that is being subtracted.
If three given seats in a stadium can be filled by any of the first five ticket holders who pass through the gate, any one of the first five gate-passing ticket-holders can fill the first of the given seats.	If any of the first five ticket-holders who pass through the gate can fill three given seats, than any one of the first five gate-passing ticket holders can fill the first of the given seats.
If a digit in a set can be repeated, any of the digits in that set can be used to fill each of the available positions if the number of positions equals the number of the digits.	If you can repeat a digit in a set, then you can use any of the digits in that set to fill any of the available positions if the number of positions equals the number of the digits.

If you've spent time reading mathematical language and being successful in math, you may find no significant difference in comprehensibility between the passive and active voice constructions. That is because you are used to this form. You don't need help in extracting meaning from it. However, the struggling math reader can find the active voice construction much more accessible: Its meaning is more direct.

I'll explain how to flip passive into active constructions in a moment, but first, you need to recognize the passive voice construction.

It is the form of the verb that determines if a sentence is set in passive or active voice. To create passive voice, we do the following:

♦ Use a form of the verb *to be* (is, am, are, was, were, be, being, been) with the form of the verb that we use with have (has, had), also know as the participle.

Let me clarify this further: The passive construction **always** has a form of the verb *to be*, and it **always** has the participle. In regular verbs, the participle looks the same as the past tense, that is, the verb plus the *ed* ending. But in irregular verbs, the participle can look all kinds of ways. Just add the auxiliary verb *have* to a verb, and you'll arrive at the participle: *have seen, have shown, have put, have brought, have found*, and so forth.

I realize that you did not pick up this book to get a grammar lesson, but you do need to understand how to flip passive voice into the more accessible active voice if you teach math. Without that teacherly skill on your part, your students won't be hearing about something that could unlock meaning for them in math text.

When the agent of the verb (action) is explicit, as it is in active voice construction, the reader finds the sentence easier to comprehend. So why do we have passive voice construction at all in the English language? Math and science writers commonly write in the passive voice when setting forth maxims because the truth that underlies the statement is true whether or not there is an agent. Writing in the passive voice has come to be a style favored by math and science writers so that they can achieve objectivity and universality.

Math language is loaded with

♦ passive voice constructions,

♦ domain-specific shifts, and

♦ chunking information in phrases.

Figure 4.3 shows words that are used in ordinary English but have a domain-specific meaning in math. To understand these words in a mathematical context, the student needs to undergo a mental shift, separating out the everyday meaning from the math-specific meaning. The savvy learner does not abandon the everyday meaning completely. To do so would be ignoring an important learning link. The idea is to see connections, using that which is familiar to access that which is new.

Figure 4.3. Domain-Specific Math Words

Acute	Area	Angle	Absolute
Associate	Base	Closure	Dependent
Argument	Circle	Cube	Even
Factor	Frequency	Identity	Like
Mean	Open	Origin	Perfect
Plane	Point	Real	Ray
Root	Sample	Statement	Stem-and-leaf
Plot	Tree	Translation	Turning point
Trend	Volume	Variable	Product
Prime			

The following are math-specific words that are used in the academic language of other subjects:

Antecedent	Rational
Oblique	Rotation
Obtuse	Sentence
Radical	Supplementary

Four Kinds of Math Reading

Now we'll take a closer look at the following four kinds of math readings common in school and their demands.

- ◆ Mathematical definitions
- ◆ Conditional statements
- ◆ Explanations of correct and wrong answers
- ◆ Procedures and directions

It's been said that you don't "read" math text, you "work" math text. You read it for immediate application to solve a problem. You work back and forth between the problem and the text, trying to get the latter to unlock the former. Much math text is definition. There are two reasons to read math definitions:

1. The defined term is used in the problem at hand.

2. The defined term is used in a new explanation of a mathematical concept.

The construction of definitions is a key concept in school. Teachers often ask for and give definitions, so that *definition language* is a kind of mini-genre all its own, and math language (especially reading and listening) is heavily dependent on formal definitions. When we hear a formal definition, we may understand it and be able to manipulate it, or we may just be able to parrot it. The latter will not help us solve a problem.

 ## Example: Mathematical Definitions

The following section covers examples of formal mathematical definitions and how we can facilitate our students' ability to really understand them.

Square root—A **square root** of a nonnegative number N is one of two equal numbers whose product is N.

Rational number—A number that can be written as a fraction with an integer numerator and a nonzero integer denominator is called a **rational number.**

Triangles—In an isosceles triangle the congruent sides are called the **legs.** The angles that are opposite the legs are called the **base angles** and, the side that they include is the **base.** The angle opposite the base is called the **vertex angle.**

Monomial/polynomial—Algebraic terms such as $7x$, $-3 \times y$, and ½ $ab2$ are called monomials. A monomial is a single number, a variable, or the product of one or more numbers and variables with positive exponents. The prefix *poly* means "many." A polynomial is an expression that contains one or more monomials: An example is $3x2 - 5x + 1$. Because polynomials represent real numbers, arithmetic operations can be performed with polynomials using the properties of real numbers.

Why a Student Might Have Difficulty Comprehending This Text

Mathematical language is dense, rich, and heavily Latinate and Greek. The reader encounters a thick forest of multisyllabic words. However, because the words are Latinate and Greek, they have components in common with other words. The key is to keep related words in the same mental compartment, using what we know to access what we don't know. The ability to mentally pronounce multisyllabic words is extremely important, so make sure that you and the students say the words aloud frequently.

You'll notice that some definitions place the target word first in the sentence and then proceed to place it in a category and then distinguish it from other members of that category. The preceding Example 1 does this. You'll notice that Example 2 does the opposite, holding off until the end of the sentence to present the target word.

Math

Either way, the *"definition sentence"* balances on the verb *is* or *is called*. Because the object in a definition sentence is not acted on by the subject but merely named, the sentence is reversible. Therefore, one mental test of comprehension is to reverse the sentence, placing the target either before or after the verb.

There are three things that one has to understand about a definition that is laid out in classical fashion (according to the pattern set forth by Aristotle):

1. What is the target word?

2. What is the general category in which the target word belongs?

3. How is the target word different from other members of its category?

Mathematical language requires us to relinquish vernacular definitions of words, and accept their domain-specific (technical) meaning. Sometimes, the term's connection to its vernacular sound-alike is too distant to be helpful (e.g., square root, rational number); other times, the mathematical term is metaphorical (e.g., leg); other times, the mathematical term is a close enough relative to its vernacular sound-alike that we can use the latter to access the former (e.g., *polynomial* is related to *poly* meaning many; *nom* meaning *name*).

So, when it comes to extracting meaning from the mathematical language used to express definitions, we can teach the student to do the following:

♦ Line the definition up (if it is not already) along classical lines: Target word, category, distinguishing characteristics.

♦ Reverse the sentence, flipping the subject and the predicate, pivoting the sentence around the *is* or *is called* verb.

♦ Consider the relationship between the mathematical term and its vernacular sound-alike.

Mini-Lesson:
Mr. Steele on Reading Mathematical Definitions

"In geometry, we have a lot of definitions, don't we? We have our own specific math definitions of words such as line, plane, point, value, and slope. We use these words in ordinary speech to mean something different from what they mean when we use them in math. In math, these words are wearing their *math uniforms.* They're working their math jobs."

> Go from known to new to understand technical terminology in math text

"Then we have those math terms that we don't use any place but math, such as trinomial, bisector, histogram, collinear. Math language has a lot of big words, but we can figure them out by recognizing parts of them, especially the parts at the beginning of the words, the prefixes. You've learned about prefixes in English. Let's look at a few of the most common prefixes that we find in math: *co-, mono-, bi-, tri- , quad-, equi-, multi-, poly-*."

"There's another kind of math term that we use; it is a phrase, which is more than one word that is taken as if it were one word. The words in the phrase stick together so closely, they form a single word in our minds such as cumulative frequency histogram, chain rule, base angles theorem, alternative interior angles, axis of symmetry."

"Let's take a look at today's homework page in the text. Let's make a list of all of the words that have math definitions, and we'll sort them into the three kinds of math vocabulary that we've been talking about."

Ordinary English Words That Have Specific Math Definitions	*Words Having a Prefix*	*Math Phrases That Act As a Single Word*

"Not every math word will fit into this chart, and some words might fit into more then one column. But this chart might help you understand how math vocabulary works."

Mr. Steele has given a simple lesson that begins to demystify mathematical language. He has taken a step toward getting students to deal head-on with math as a matter of language rather than math as a matter of numbers and symbols only. He will repeat this mini-lesson, having students add to their columns as they meet new terms. As the year progresses, Mr. Steele's students will constantly revisit their "math language table," increasing their understanding about the following essential concepts:

♦ Words have domain-specific meanings that are usually, but not necessarily, obviously related to their vernacular meanings.

♦ Polysyllabic words can be broken down by their familiar parts (prefixes and, later, roots).

♦ Domain-specific phrases need to be understood as a whole.

 ## Example: Conditional Statements

A good deal of math reading comes in the form of conditional statements, also called syllogisms, or the well-known *if/then* statements. The following text explains the three kinds of conditional statements.

> Two statements can be linked together to form a conditional statement by writing, "*If* statement 1, *then* statement 2." There are three related conditional statements that can be formed: the converse, inverse, and contrapositive.
>
> In the conditional statement "If statement p, then statement q," statement p is called the hypothesis (or antecedent) and statement q is called the conclusion (or consequent). A conditional is always true except if the hypothesis (statement p) is true and, at the same time, the conclusion (statement q) is false. Here is an example:
>
> If x is a multiple of 4, then x is a multiple of 3.
>
> The truth of this conditional statement depends on the replacement value of x.
>
> ♦ Given x = 12
>
>   If 12 is a multiple of 4, then 12 is a multiple of 3.
>
> The hypothesis and the conclusion are both true. Therefore, the conditional statement is true.
>
> ♦ Given x = 8
>
>   If 8 is a multiple of 4, then 8 is a multiple of 3.
>
> The hypothesis is true, but the conclusion is false. Therefore, the conditional statement is false.
>
> ♦ Given x = 9
>
>   If 9 is a multiple of 4, then 9 is a multiple of 3.
>
> The hypothesis is false, but the conclusion is true. Therefore, the conditional statement is true.

> ◆ Given $x = 7$
>
> If 7 is a multiple of 4, then 7 is a multiple of 3.
>
> The hypothesis and the conclusion are both false. Therefore, the conditional statement is true.

Why a Student Might Have Difficulty Comprehending This Text

The difficult part of reading this information is that the reader has to hold onto tentative ideas to determine realities. Think about how different that mental state is from, let's say, social studies reading where the facts parade along with the reader taking in the sights. Yes, it is true that social studies readers need to exert critical thinking, but when you read social studies material, you aren't conjuring up hypothetical conditions, as you are here.

The math reader needs to be thinking: I'm learning a maxim that I will have to apply to other conditions that are not laid out as explicitly as this one is. The math reader will encounter *hidden* conditionals in which the language does not conform to the if/then pattern, such as Figure 4.4.

Figure 4.4. Hidden Conditionals

Equivalent Forms of a Conditional	*Example*
If p, then q	If it is Wednesday, then I have a dentist's appointment.
P implies q	It being Wednesday implies that I have a dentist's appointment.
Q if p	I have a dentist's appointment if it is Wednesday.
P only if q	I have a dentist's appointment only if it is Wednesday.

Mathematical knowledge is based on cumulative understandings. Only if a math reader understands the foregoing can he or she proceed to the following permutations of the conditional statement.

Converse, Inverse, and Contrapositive Statements

The **converse** of a conditional statement is formed by reversing the hypothesis with the conclusion. The **inverse** of a conditional statement is formed by making both the hypothesis and the conclusion *negative*. The **contrapositive** of a conditional statement, is formed by doing both of what the converse and the inverse formations do: reversal and negation of the hypothesis and the conclusion. This information is likely to be unclear until an example is provided.

Conditional: If it is Wednesday, then I have a dentist's appointment.

Converse: If I have a dentist's appointment, then it is Wednesday.

Inverse: If it is not Wednesday, then I do not have a dentist's appointment.

Contrapositive: If I do not have a dentist appointment, then it is not Wednesday.

We can see that math text of this nature is all about the patterns and can therefore be accessed if the reader makes visual organizers to follow the pattern.

Mini-Lesson:
Mrs. Artuso on Reading Conditional Statements

"In math, we're always hearing, *if/then* statements, aren't we? These happen to be called conditional statements, or syllogisms, but we can just call them *if/then* statements for now. You didn't just start hearing *if/then* statements in this class. You've been hearing them all your life. Think back to when you were little. Did your parents give you *if/then* statements? What were they?"

> Go from known to new to understand a mathematical syllogism

Student responses may sound like these:

"If you kids don't stop fighting, I'm turning this car right around, and we're not going."

"If you complain about not having enough candy one more time, I'm taking it all away."

"If you eat all your Brussels sprouts, you can have dessert. Otherwise, no dessert."

"If it rains, we'll have the party inside."

Mrs. Artuso writes these responses on the board: "So we can see that these are *if/then* statements even though there is no *then*. The *then* can be implied. What do all these statements have in common besides that they all begin with *if*?"

"Something is going to happen."

"You have to do this or you get that."

"They have two parts to them."

"Okay, good. We see a pattern. Let's call the *if* part the *premise*. *Pre-* means before." She underlines the premises of the examples on the board. "And let's call the *then* part the conclusion." She circles the conclusions.

From these simple, real-life examples that summon prior knowledge, Mrs. Artuso is able to build understanding of an essential math concept, the conditional statement. From here, she reverses and negates the clauses of the familiar statements to show the formation of the converse, inverse, and contrapositive.

She says, "We're going to be working a lot with conditional statements. When you get lost in them, remember the conditional statements that you heard when you were little and how easy it was for you to understand them. The form, which is the frame of the conditional statements is the same. It's the variables, the specific details, that are different."

Explanations of Correct and Wrong Answers:

1. In a bag of 50 buttons, 18 are red, 26 are green, and 2 are both red and green. How many buttons in the bag are neither either red or green?

   a. 6
   b. 8
   c. 16
   d. 24

   The correct answer is (b). A good way to find the answer to this problem is to draw a Venn Diagram (overlapping circles) representing the red and green buttons. The circle for red buttons has the number 18; the circle for green buttons has the number 26. These two circles overlap. You would draw a third circle that overlaps the other two circles. This third overlapping circle represents the 2 red and green buttons. Because you do not want to count the red and green buttons twice, you would subtract 2 from either the red or the green group. Adding all values (24 + 16 + 2) gives a total of 42 buttons. (Note that the 2 red and green buttons have been subtracted from the green group.) Therefore, in the bag of 50 buttons, 8 are neither red or green.

   Why are the wrong answers wrong? If you chose (a) as the answer, you may have counted the mixed colored buttons twice and subtracted 44 from 50 to arrive at the number 6. If you chose (c) or (d) as the answer, you may have understood that you needed to subtract 2 (for the mixed colored buttons) from either the red or green group, but you did not add the total number of red, green, mixed colored buttons and then subtract that sum from the total number of buttons to arrive at the number of buttons *not* included in the Venn diagram.

Math

2. What is true about the statement "If two angles are right angles, the angles have equal measure" and its converse "If two angles have equal measure then the two angles are right angles"?

    a. The statement is true but its converse is false.

    b. The statement is false but its converse is true.

    c. Both the statement and its converse are false.

    d. Both the statement and its converse are true.

The correct answer is (a). Because all right angles have 90 degrees, all right angles are of equal measure. However, two angles can be equal in measure (each being 30 degrees), but they are not necessarily right angles. The converse is the reversal of the hypothesis (the *if* clause) and the conclusion (the *then* clause)

Why are the wrong answers wrong? Any of the wrong answers can indicate that you don't understand what is meant by the converse of a conditional statement.

 ### Example: Procedures and Directions

A linear-quadratic system of equations such as $x + y = 1$ and $y = -x2 + 4x - 3$ can be solved algebraically as follows in Figure 4.5:

Figure 4.5. Solving an Equation

Step	Example
1. Rewrite the linear equation, expressing one of the variables in terms of the other, if this is possible.	$x + y = 1$ $y = -x + 1$
2. Take the expression just obtained and substitute it into the quadratic equation by solving for the variable in the linear equation.	Because $y = -x + 1$, replace y by same: $y = -x2 + 4x - 3$ $-x + 1 = x2 + 4x - 3$
3. Using standard form, express a quadratic equation, and solve it.	$0 = -x2 + 4x + x - 3 - 1$ $0 = -x2 + 5x - 4$ Multiply each term by -1: $0 = x2 - 5x + 4$ $0 = (x - 1)(x - 4)$ $x - 1 = 0$ or $x - 4 = 0$ $x = 1;$ $x = 4$

4. Substitute each root of the quadratic equation into the linear equation to find the value of the remaining variable of each ordered pair.	Let $x = 1$; Then $y = -x + 1$; $= -1 + 1$ $= 0$	Let $x = 4$ Then $y = -x + 1$ $= -4 + 1$ $= -3$
	The solution set is $\{(1,0), (4,-3)\}$	
5. Check your work: Verify that each ordered pair satisfies each of the original equations.		

Why a Student Might Have Difficulty Comprehending This Text

Even though there are examples to illustrate the text, there is a lot of abstract mathematical phraseology whose meaning is assumed. For example, the student might not understand what *in terms of the other* means, despite the example. The word *express* might not translate to *write*, which is what the solver has to do to express something in math. The words *the expression just obtained* simply means the *answer to the procedure that you just did*, but that might not be evident. Needless to say, the reader who would not understand those basics would in no way be able to make sense of this text.

In procedural text, we have a series of verbs that tell us what to do. We have to identify the verbs and make sure that we know what each means. The verbs in the previous procedure are: *rewrite, express,* and *substitute*. Math life is difficult for students with poor math reading skills. Whether students need to review concepts taught through lecture in class, read information for the first time, understand procedures and directions, or unpack a word problem, students need to read math, and reading math is something that they are probably not taught explicitly to do. The math teacher can wrongly assume that all of the necessary math reading skills have been taught by the English teacher. The English teacher may never have given a moment's thought to the reading skills necessary for math or to the convergence and divergence of language between English and math.

Comparing Math Language to the Language of Other Subjects

Math language, perhaps more than any other subject, is understood not through single words but through phrases. Think of math language as a mix-and-match kit in which we put together words to make phrases such as: *absolute value, least common denominator, greatest common multiple.*

More than other subjects, math reading involves reading nonalphabetical symbols. These symbols represent numbers, operations, relationships, and organizational structures of information (charts, tables, graphs). We also have symbols that don't appear anywhere else: infinity, radicals, square roots. The symbols, although they don't have a sound-to-symbol (phonic) relationship, do have to be treated as reading issues because they are symbolic and therefore involve decoding.

What Kind of Reading is Expected in Business, Computer, and Vocational Classes?

Reading for business is a cross between reading for math and reading for social studies. You have a lot of numerical information, much of it graphically expressed, but you also have language having legal characteristics, and that means a lot of Latin prefixes and roots. Business language employs a lot of words that take on specific meanings, apart from their vernacular meanings, such as: *security, deposit, clause, renewal, speculate, consideration.* And business documents favor legal-sounding words such as pursuant to, hereinafter, and whereas that students might not be accustomed to.

Business language found in legal documents tends to be Latinate and stodgy, whereas computer language tends to be youthful and lively. Either way, like any specialized field, the students has to acclimate to the diction of the field. We call diction that characterizes a particular field jargon. Getting used to the jargon is part of domain-specific learning. As novices, we're tongue-tied, and need a lot of exposure and examples to acclimate to jargon. As with any new language, whether that be a bona fide foreign language, or a new style of our native language, we understand the spoken word when we hear it before we can produce it in speech by ourselves. And, of course, we learn words in chunks and clusters.

Consider how the following terms are used in a business, as opposed to a vernacular, context.

Term of the lease	Representation
Conditions of the lease	Agency
Security deposit	Expiration
Set down	Permit
Retire	Party

When we consider the importance of prior knowledge in reading comprehension, we come to a stumbling block for reading about business, money, and things that cost money (such as computers). Students who grow up in families where there is little or no disposable income or income that is invested are going to lack prior knowledge when it comes to reading about interest, tax deductions, return versus risk, stocks and bonds, and other basic information about money that they don't have and don't hear about at home. Think about how advantaged, not only financially but in terms of knowledge about finances, the student is who comes from a family where such language is in the air. It can be hard for some of your students to even imagine having so much money that you have to learn about how to invest it, much less to understand a vocabulary of such wealth. Ironically, of course, it is just these students who need business and financial education the most.

Business students learn about organizational systems that can be as simple and small as a teenager's management of his or her allowance and income from a part-time job to as large and complex as a major corporation. Both systems can be represented graphically.

Business students also learn about marketing and consumerism, economics, ethics, the law, computers, personal goal-setting, and communication styles. A lot of classifying goes on, as students learn about exemplars and adaptations in different fields of business.

To be a good reader in a business education class, the student has to be a good holistic thinker: most business text depends on the understanding of a big picture: a system, an organization, an overall plan that has steps that can change depending on conditions. The instructional implication for good business reading is to have students translate paragraphed information into graphic representations and vice versa.

Example: Business Education

> Our sales forecast for the next quarter will form the basis for our financial plans for the remainder of the current fiscal year. From the sales forecast, we will develop production plans. The production plans will arise from considerations of costs of raw materials and lead times. We will use the production plans to estimate such factors as labor costs and requirements, factory overhead, and office expenses. We will then prepare our cash budget. At that point, we will be able to develop our final income statement and balance sheet.

Why a Student Might Have Difficulty Comprehending This Text

Let me point out something about this language, a feature that typifies business language: We have a lot of phrases in which the adjective is really a noun. This makes for dense reading. The examples in the preceding reading are: *sales forecast* (sales is a noun here used to modify forecast), *production plans, labor costs, factory overhead, office expenses, cash budget, balance sheet.* We don't have to mention that the text is dense because of so many double-noun phrases, but the phrase *production plans* appears multiple times, and it would be a good idea to factor it out: What exactly do we mean by production plans?

Mini-Lesson:
Mrs. Koch on After-Reading, Meaning-Making Activity

"What we're reading here is something that business people read all the time: a systematic project plan. To help us understand it, draw a

> Use a graphic representation to clarify text

flow chart that shows the steps of the plan. Then, to make sure that you really understand it, talk about how a change in any one of the steps would affect the whole project, and what you might do to set things right."

By asking for this kind of paragraph-to-graphic processing, Mrs. Koch is wisely employing a key mode of communication in the business world, the flow chart. She's also fortified the activity by having students come up with a Plan B for the not-so-unlikely event that the unexpected will happen to disrupt the business plan.

Reading for Computer and Vocational Education

The language of computer education is largely metaphorical. Some of the metaphors, such as *mouse*, are named for obvious similarities between the finger-operated cursor-control device and the rodent for whom it is named. Other metaphors in the easy-to-understand category include *home page, thumbnail, wizard, bins, desktop*. Others, such as *cookie*, to identify a file of information about a visitor to a particular Web site, are more obscure in their metaphorical meaning. Computer language is loaded with acronyms (JPEG, GIF, HTML, FTP, URL) and brand names treated as common nouns (Microsoft Access, Microsoft Excel, Microsoft Power Point, Microsoft Word, Adobe). Then there is a set of verbs for what an operator of a computer might do: *copy, paste, group, ungroup, tab, input*. As you can see, some of these are metaphorical as well, and most have undergone a usage shift from noun to verb. Finally, we have words that have hopped over from mathematics: *query, data, sort, argument, mean*. Left over are words from the realm of electronics: *modem, cursor, microprocessor*.

Like the language of computer education, that of vocational education is loaded with technical and metaphorical terms. In vocational education classes, the reading that students are expected to do is usually immediately applicable to a task at hand: reading that answers the question, "What am I supposed to do with the tools in front of me?"

A lot of the reading consists of labeled figures, so the reader has to be able to mentally translate a drawing of, let's say, a car engine, to the actual item. Although the actual item is three-dimensional and can be looked at from various perspectives, the drawing shows only one side, often a cross-section. It is not necessarily an easy task to understand how a cross-section drawing represents a real object that you are used to seeing and holding.

What business, computer, and vocational education have in common is that they all call for the understanding of a system. Nouns, often polysyllabic or metaphorical ones, name the parts of the system. The student must come to understand the relationship among the discrete parts, how the system breaks down when one of the relationships fails, and the extent to which an individual can control the system. In all three cases, the student must learn how to communicate about the system to others whose understanding is greater than theirs.

 Example: Vocational Education

Optical Disks

Videodisks, also called optical disks, make possible all kinds of new applications because of their storage capacity. They can store video images, audio, text, and data. Optical disk systems use light energy to store data. (Magnetic disk systems use magnetic fields to store data. Videodisks use one of two methods to have a high-powered laser beam store data. The first method is called the ablative method. In the ablative method, the laser beam burns a hole in the surface of the disk. The other method is called the bubble method. In the bubble method, a bubble forms when the disk surface is heated.

Then, the laser beam, in a lower power mode, is capable of reading the data by sensing the presence or absence of bumps or holes. The resulting different angles that are formed from the disfigured or flat surface reflects the light. Then, the light beam is reflected by a series of mirrors onto a photodiode. That is how the light energy transforms into an electric signal. If you've ever walked through an automatic door at a supermarket, you've experienced this sequence. What happens is that you deflect a light beam as you walk through the door. That deflection causes the door to open.

Why Students Might Have Difficulty Comprehending This Text

This text is used to explain how machinery works in a vocational or a computer class. Its concepts are about physics and forces that we can't see or feel directly: light energy, magnetic fields, electronic storage. The student who approaches this text having experience with disks and e-storage will be in position to understand its main point: how optical disk technology represents an advancement in disk technology. The most important word in this text is arguably *deflection*.

Mini-Lesson: Mr. Davis on After-Reading

Use a graphic representation to clarify text

Mr. Davis presents his strategy for tying up information with a graphic representation.

"A lot of what we read here is about how things work. It's one thing to read the words about how something works, but you have to do something after you read to really have it sink in. Let's read this piece about how optical disks work and then pretend that it's our job to make a diagram for the textbook company to help students understand it. Let's start by scanning for words that we want to know more about." Mr. Davis solicits several key words from the text and writes them on the board. Most of the words have component parts that yield meaning, and Mr. Davis explains how to analyze them: *photo,* meaning light; *deflect,* with the root *flect* meaning bend; *optical,* with the root *opt,* meaning related to the eyes. Mr. Davis regularly breaks down words believing that it is an important enough skill to justify the time it takes to attend to it.

"What we're going to do is to read the information, and then work with a partner to come up with a diagram. Then, your partnership will explain your diagram to another partnership, and they'll explain theirs to you."

This is a simple, effective paradigm for making meaning out of information that relies on a technical language to explain a procedure that can't be observed by the naked eye. The students enter the text knowing key words, they have a motivation to read carefully (a partner), they have a clear task to carry out, and meaningful follow-up on it.

What Kind of Reading Is Expected in Science Class?

Science text has a great deal of graphic information, such as tables and charts, as well as photographs and illustration. As with math text and language acquisition text, the reader is expected to make meaning by using both the paragraphed text and the graphic information. In science, some of the graphic information, such as weather maps are authentic, meaning that professionals in the field might be using the same maps. Most of the information that students read in science is inauthentic, meaning that someone has written it not to advance the field of science, but to explain science to students in a particular grade level.

The advantage of inauthentic text is that it has been tailored to meet the reading needs of school-aged youngsters. The vocabulary is carefully doled out, the textual features are there to support reading comprehension, and the explanations assume no prior knowledge except that which has been cumulatively learned within the text. It contains reader aids such as chapter summaries, a glossary, headings, and subheadings.

The disadvantage of inauthentic text is that it is bland, so as not to offend the large numbers of school districts that the publisher hopes will use it. As teachers, we may or may not appreciate the lack of controversy, but it's difficult to get students interested in straightforward facts devoid of a point of view.

 ## Example: Science Textbook

Here are some examples of what students are expected to read in Earth Science classes and commentary on why they might have difficulty.

Three Kinds of Rocks

Igneous   Sedimentary   Metamorphic

Igneous Rocks

Formation:

Molten rock, called *magma*, solidifies deep within the Earth. The final rock type is determined by the *chemical composition* of the magma and the *rate at which it cooled.*

Kinds of:

Intrusive and *Extrusive*

About the two kinds of igneous rocks:

Intrusive igneous rocks, also called *plutonic* rocks, are magma-formed rocks that have cooled very slowly from deep within the Earth. The reason for the slow cooling rate is that surrounding rocks provided insulation. Because of the slow cooling rate, the mineral grains had a long time to grow, and so these mineral grains tend to be large and coarse.

Extrusive igneous rocks, also called *volcanic* rocks, are magma-formed rocks whose cooling has taken place close to the Earth's surface. The solidifying process, being close to the water and air, was relatively rapid. Because of the speed of the solidifying (cooling) process, volcanic rocks are fine-grained. Volcanic glass—rock whose grain is so fine as to be unrecognizable as a grainy substance—is formed when the cooling process is so rapid that individual grains do not have time to grow enough to form grains.

The word *igneous* is related to the word *ignite,* meaning *to catch fire,* because these rocks were formed through volcanic fires.

Sedimentary Rocks

Formation:

Pieces of dead organisms and other rocks form sedimentary rocks out of deposits that solidify through pressure on the surface of the Earth.

Kinds of:

Clastic, Chemical, Biologic

About the three kinds of sedimentary rock:

Clastic Sedimentary Rocks:

Pieces of rocks that already existed before becoming sedimentary rocks are called clastics. These clastics were loosened by forces such as water and weathering. After they were loosened, they traveled and became trapped in a depression somewhere. There, it compressed and formed sedimentary rock. There is a large variation in grain size to be found in clastic sedimentary rocks. You can find grains that you can't see with the naked eye, right up to "grains" the size of large boulders. The key characteristic of clastic sedimentary rock is that it formed from preexisting rock that was transported and then transformed in its new environment.

Chemical Sedimentary Rocks:

The process known as chemical precipitation forms chemical sedimentary rocks. Chemical precipitation occurs when water travels through rocks, taking minerals with it, transporting these minerals away from their original rocks. When the water evaporates or becomes oversaturated with minerals, these minerals re-form, in another place. The re-formed minerals create chemical sedimentary rocks.

Biologic Sedimentary Rocks:

As you might expect, biologic sedimentary rocks are formed from organisms that were once living. Plant life and animal life, including shells, form biologic sedimentary rocks.

The word sedimentary is related to other words having the Latin root *sed* or *sid*, meaning *sit. (sediment, sedentary, preside, president, consider).*

Metamorphic Rocks

Formation:

We call rocks metamorphic when they have changed substantially from their previous forms. Their previous forms can have been igneous, sedimentary, or older metamorphic. When rocks are affected by extreme temperatures, extreme pressure, mineral or chemical-rich fluids, great changes can occur. If such changes are so great as to bring about a substantially new kind of rock, then the new kind of rock is considered metamorphic.

> **Kinds of:**
>
> *Foliated* or *Non-foliated*
>
> **About the two kinds of metamorphic rocks:**
>
> *Foliated Metamorphic Rocks:*
>
> Foliation is the process of minerals forming sheets, or plates, that align as a result of extreme pressure. The foliation will reflect the direction of the pressure.
>
> *Non-Foliated Metamorphic Rocks:*
>
> As you would expect, non-foliated metamorphic rocks have not been sheeted by pressure, but that is not to say that pressure has not been applied to them. Rocks such as limestone do not have the kind of minerals that are going to foliate (align). Some rocks become metamorphic because of heat: The heat can be so great as to alter the mineral structure to such an extent that a new kind of rock is created.
>
> You might recognize the *morph* part of the word *metamorphic. Morph* means change.

Why a Student Might Have Difficulty Comprehending This Text

I see vocabulary issues here, although the text does try to make the big words easier by explaining their Latin roots. Another comprehension barrier can be the sheer unfamiliarity and lack of interest and exposure that a student can feel toward the subject of rock classification. (Although, to this day, despite not being a science person or a rock-climbing person or even an outdoorsy person, I hold clear memories of rocks that we passed around for identification purposes in ninth-grade earth science lab. I do like rocks when properly set in 14-carat gold, but it was the visual and tactile experience that made one science lesson durable for me.)

Actually, this is reader-friendly text. The student who has difficulty with it may not be hooking up with its many patterns and cues. Notice the parallel way in which the information is presented. This text would translate well into a visual organizer or outline.

What Kind of Reading Is Expected in Social Studies Class?

As with a science textbook, a social studies textbook consists of mostly inauthentic text in that it isn't history, but someone's explanation of history. Increasingly, students are asked to read primary source documents, and that is authentic

Social Studies

text that presents a different kind of reading problem. When reading primary source documents, the reader has to "double read": What I mean by that is that the reader has to read the information and consider that information in light of its historical significance. Not to do the latter is to miss the point of the former. Primary source documents present language challenges of archaic sentence structure and vocabulary. Some, such as slave narratives, diaries, and letters, can even be written in authentic dialect, which can be hard to decode.

Example: Social Studies Textbook

The sample text that follows is typical of what might be found in a social studies textbook. It will be followed by a primary source document. Note the difference.

> Perhaps nothing demonstrates the industry, thoroughness, and engineering skill of the Romans better than the system of roads with which they linked their empire. Built like walls as much as three feet deep into the ground and running in straight lines across all but the most difficult terrain, many of these roads are still in use today. They are more than monuments to Roman building skills; they are testimony to the practical vision of a people who quickly saw that their military conquests would be made permanent and that commerce and colonization would flourish only with an extensive and efficient means of communication. The Roman army, under the supervision of engineers, built much of the nearly fifty thousand miles of hard-surface highways—enough to circle the globe twice—radiating out from Rome through Italy and beyond. For a faster means of travel, the world had to wait until the eighteenth century when the invention of the steam engine made railroads and steamships possible. The construction of our railroads is a better parallel to the Romans' efforts than our present system of superhighways, for westward expansion was supported initially by the railway system. Even now, well over two thousand years after the Romans built many of their roads, America's system of interstate highways is still being completed.

Why a Student Might Have Difficulty Comprehending This Text

Long paragraphs can be difficult because they demand that sustained focus. Many of the sentences here are not only long but have delayed subjects, requiring the reader to process introductory information before being able to subconsciously link subject and verb to click the sentence together. As far as the overall meaning is concerned, the reader has to understand that the passage is about the marvel of the

Roman roads, not the American railroads, steamships, or interstate highway systems. Those examples are there in service to the main idea (Roman roads).

 # Example: Reading a Primary Source Document

Following is a sample primary source document from "A Short Narrative of the Horrid Massacre in Boston" by James Bowdoin, Dr. Joseph Warren, and Samuel Pemberson (1770).

> The actors in this dreadful tragedy were a party of soldiers commanded by Captain Preston of the 29th regiment. This party, including the captain, consisted of eight, who are all committed to jail.
>
> There are depositions in this affair which mention, that several guns were fired at the same time from the Custom House; before which this shocking scene was exhibited. Into this matter inquisition is now making. In the meantime it may be proper to insert here the substance of some of those depositions.
>
> Benjamin Frizell, on the evening of the 5th of March, having taken his station near the west corner of the Custom House in King Street, before and at the time of the soldiers firing their guns, declares (among other things) that the first discharge was only of one gun, the next of two guns, on which he the deponent thinks he saw two men fall; and immediately after were discharged five guns, two of which were by soldiers on his right hand; the other three, as appeared to the deponent, were discharged from the balcony, or the chamber window of the Custom House, the flashes appearing on the left hand, and higher than the right hand flashes appeared to be, and of which the deponent was very sensible, although his eyes were much turned to the soldiers, who were all on his right hand.

Why a Student Might Have Difficulty Comprehending This Text

Some of the archaic syntax can be off-putting ("Into this matter inquisition is now making.") and the reader might not be able to picture a Custom House, a key visual in this narrative. It would be interesting to pair this passage side by side against the textbook description of the event to compare how the language and the details affect the reader.

Of course, if the reader didn't know anything about the significance of the Boston Massacre, this narrative would have little meaning beyond the obvious. For it to have meaning, the reader must be aware of the import of the street shootings that came to be known as the Boston Massacre.

Example: Reading a Primary Source Document Written in Dialect

Here is another sort of primary source document from *Lay My Burden Down* by Jenny Proctor (1945).

> I's hear tell of them good slave days, but I ain't never seen no good times then. My mother's name was Lisa, and when I was a very small child I hear that driver going from cabin to cabin as early as 3 o'clock in the morning, and when he comes to our cabin he say, "Lisa, Lisa, git up from there and git that breakfast." My mother, she was cook, and I don't recollect nothing 'bout my father. If I had any brothers and sisters I didn't know it. We had old ragged huts made out of poles and some of the cracks chinked up with mud and moss and some of them wasn't. We didn't have no good beds, just scaffolds nailed up to the wall out of poles and the old ragged bedding throwed on them. That sure was hard sleeping, but even that feel good to our weary bones after them long hard days' work in the field. I tended to the children when I was a little gal and tried to clean the house just like Old Miss tells me to. Then soon as I was ten years old, Old Master, he say, "Git in the cotton patch."

Where a Student Might Have Difficulty Comprehending This Text

This writer writes in dialect, and although it's rather accessible compared to some representations of dialect, it can get in the way of comprehension. The reader needs to hear the writer's voice, accent, style of speech to get the sense of authenticity of the text: This is a real person speaking in her own voice.

What Kind of Reading Is Expected in Classes for Languages Other Than English?

For the purpose of uniformity, I'll use the example of classes in Latin. In language-learning classes, there are two kinds of reading. The first is authentic text, in which students are reading just as a speaker of the target language would read. This would include literary text, signage, menus, newspapers, and other text that a native speaker might read. The second kind of reading, and that is the reading that I'll be talking about, is text written in English that explains the grammatical rules and lexicon of the target language. Much of that kind of text is what we call "process analysis"; that is, it explains how to do something, step by step, much as a mathematics text might do.

In the textbook, we have a lot of explanation and examples. In fact, the language-learning textbook is not dissimilar to the mathematics text in that the reader needs to go back and forth between the models and the explanations, and then between the models and explanations and the practice exercises that require application of the explanations according to the models. In addition to this type of text, we also have information, often side-lined in a box, about the culture of native speakers of the target language. In that sense, language-learning text is similar to social studies text. And most language-learning textbooks also include some authentic literature in the target language, similar to that which would be read in English class. This type of reading becomes more lengthy and frequent in the upper levels, until the student is reading mostly authentic literature in the language-learning class.

To be successful as a reader in the earlier years of learning a new language, the reader must know the purpose for reading. Reading about how to conjugate irregular verbs is not pleasure reading (for most folks) but functional reading, reading to learn how to do a specific thing. Without immediate application this kind reading will be instantly forgotten. And the reader has to read with her *comparison/contrast* hat on because she needs to bring forth what she already knows about English to learn how the target language is the same and different from it, grammatically and lexically.

Example: Foreign Language Textbook

Here are two examples, word order and tense, from a Latin textbook, and the challenges that they might present.

> **Word Order in Latin and English**
>
> The order in which words appear in a sentence to make meaning is what we call *word order*. Languages treat word order differently. How word order conveys meaning in a sentence is a significant difference between Latin and English. In English, the connection between words in a sentence is shown by word order; but in Latin, that connection is shown not by word order, but by word endings. English is considered a *word order* language; Latin is considered an *inflected* language. By inflected, we mean that the words change their form, usually by adding endings.
>
> In English, the sentences, *James leads Francis,* and *Francis leads James* have two different meanings. But in Latin, you could say either *James dūcit Francis,* or *Francis dūcit James,* and have the same meaning conveyed.

Another word order difference between Latin and English has to do with where adjectives are placed in the sentence, relative to the nouns that they modify. In English, we generally find the adjective preceding the noun: the *sly* fox. But in Latin, it's the opposite: The adjectives generally follow the nouns that they modify. However, in Latin, adjectives of size (*magnum*) generally precede the nouns that they modify.

Where a Student Might Have Difficulty Comprehending This Text

This text is best understood through the generation of examples. If you understand its point about word order and inflectional differences between Latin and English, then you can generate an infinite number of examples in English in which the subject and the direct object are distinguishable based on word order, and how the meaning is not retained when the subject and the direct object are switched. Similarly, the reader has to be able to generate an infinite number of examples of pre-noun adjectives.

That English is a word order language, and Latin is an inflected language is absolutely key to foundational understandings of Latin, as we learn it as a nonnative language. Yet, the reader has probably never thought about the word order nature of English. We grow up speaking a language, absorbing its rules, without ever realizing that those rules may not apply to other languages. In that sense, this bit of text should deliver a revelation to students who are learning a Romance language for the first time. If they're not astonished by the fact that you can move words around in Latin without altering the meaning significantly, as you would in English, then they probably don't understand what this bit of text is saying.

However, even though we are receiving astonishing information, we are reading very dry, matter-of-fact language. There's dissonance between the excitement of the message—its power to astonish—and the nonexcitement of the writer's voice. That dissonance can be a stumbling block to comprehension.

The Perfect Tense

In English, we use the past tense to refer to an action that is over and done: *He ate pizza for lunch yesterday*. We used the present perfect tense to refer to an action that began in the past and may be continuing into the present, or, it may have occurred over a nonspecific time in the past, or in the very recent past: *He has just eaten pizza*. One does not say *He has eaten pizza yesterday*.

In Latin, we use the perfect tense for *both* the past and the present perfect of English. Most of the time, we use the perfect tense in Latin the way the past tense is used in English:

Grātiam meruimus. We deserved (have deserved) gratitude.

Magister paellās docuit. The teacher taught (has taught) the girls.

Viam spectāvimus. We looked (have looked) at the road.

Perfect Tense and Perfect Stem

The verbs that we've studied so far form the perfect tense in the first conjugation by adding –v– to the present stem: *līberā-, līberāv-*. To form the perfect stem of verbs of the second conjugation, we would drop the –ī of the perfect first person singular, which is the third principal part of the verb (as listed in your lesson vocabulary list), *doceō, docēre, docuī, doctus: docu-*. To form the perfect tense, we would add the perfect tense endings to the perfect stem.

Why a Student Might Have Difficulty Comprehending This Text

This is a time where a certain piece of prior knowledge is not going to be helpful because the word *perfect* in grammar does not mean what it means in vernacular English. Grammatically, the word *perfect* actually refers to completeness of action. Because you are a foreign language teacher, you have long ago become comfortable with this terminology. You no longer attribute the vernacular meaning of *perfect* to its grammatical meaning. But you probably did just that when you first heard the word *perfect* applied to verbs.

This text refers directly to certain pieces of prior knowledge about how Latin grammar works, so if the reader were in the dark about that information, that would certainly impede comprehension.

The textual pattern here, as in a great deal of foreign language textbook readings, is process analysis: The text is giving you directions about how to do something, step by step. When we read process analysis, we need to focus on two things:

1. Verbs: The verbs are telling you what to do.

2. Reasons: When we read process analysis, to really comprehend, we need to know not only what to do, but also why we are doing it. When it comes to learning a language, the reasons why we do certain things grammatically are because we are following rules to create the language pattern. The steps in the process follow the pattern that conforms to the rule.

This is a good example of text that must be read for a specific purpose. No one reads about how to form verb tenses in another language because they wish to while away the hours on a summer afternoon by the lake. The reader must establish a very practical purpose for this information: "I'm reading this because I need to know how to create the perfect tense in Latin." Only with that definite purpose in mind does the text deliver its intended meaning.

What Kind of Reading Is Expected in English Class

It is in English class that most people expect secondary school reading to be taught. Yet, if we look at the kind of reading that students do in English class, we see how different it is from reading in the other subject areas. My purpose in discussing English class reading last is to have you note this difference and to have you understand why it is so important for teachers other than English teachers to address domain-specific reading issues, and why English teachers have to include expository text as well as literary text if they are to improve reading skills that will make a lifelong difference.

For one thing, we've seen how heavily the other subject areas depend on textual features and graphic information along with the words of reading. A student doesn't learn this kind of reading skill in an English class. A novel, for example, has few textual features to inform the reader of its meaning. There are almost no tables, charts, and labeled diagrams in English class. Numbers and symbols are not integrated into reading in English class.

For another, English class readings are mostly narrative and descriptive, whereas, for the rest of the school day, the student is reading cause and effect and comparison/contrast pattern clusters. This makes a big difference in reader focus, expectation, and processing.

But the most important difference between English class, literary text, and expository text has to do with implication. Literary text is highly connotative and subtle. The reader has to read for unspoken truths. The reader of literary text acts as an observer of human events, human events that are subject to various responses and interpretations. Much literary text is designed to be puzzling, and that is *not* what expository text is designed for. The reader of literary text is always supposed to be asking: "Should I be trusting the person who is telling me this story, or am I supposed to read above and beyond the narrator's voice to see what's really going on here?"

Literary text, unlike expository text, is meant to meander, inviting the reader to linger over episodes and turns of phrase. Where expository text is meant to be read efficiently, literary text is meant to be read, shall we say, *languorously*. Languorous reading is something that most students are not wont to do (not that they are so wont to do efficient reading, either, hence this book).

 # Example: Reading Fiction

The following are two examples: The first is an excerpt from *The Masque of the Red Death* by Edgar Allan Poe.

> It was a blue room where stood the prince, with a group of pale courtiers by his side. At first, as he spoke, there was a slight rushing movement of this group in the direction of the intruder, who at the moment was also near at hand, and now, with deliberate and stately step, made closer approach to the speaker. But from a certain nameless awe with which the mad assumptions of the mummer had inspired the whole party, there were found none who put forth hand to seize him; so that, unimpeded, he passed within a yard of the prince's person; and, while the vast assembly, as if with one impulse, shrank from the centers of the rooms to the walls, he made his step which had distinguished him from the first, through the blue chamber to the purple—through the purple to the green—through the green to the orange—through this again to the white—and even thence to the violet, ere a decided movement had been made to arrest him.

Why a Student Might Have Difficulty Comprehending This Text

This is what I mean by text that is meant to be read languorously. The sentences are long, drawing the reader into a swirl of phrases. The adjectives occasionally follow the noun, ("…unimpeded, he passed…") causing the reader to slow down. And we have grammatical inversions ("where stood the prince") that also have the effect of slowing pace. In addition, the reader is meant to question the reality of the situation being described: Poe's writing has a dream-like quality. This literary text creates a world of make-believe that is not found in expository text.

Example: Poetry

For the second example, let's go with the introductory verse of the famous narrative poem by Henry Wadsworth Longfellow, "Evangeline."

> THIS is the forest primeval. The murmuring pines and the hemlocks,
>
> Bearded with moss, and in garments green, indistinct in the twilight,
>
> Stand like Druids of eld, with voices sad and prophetic,
>
> Stand like harpers hoar, with beards that rest on their bosoms.
>
> Loud from its rocky caverns, the deep-voiced neighboring ocean
>
> Speaks, and in accents disconsolate answers the wail of the forest.
>
> This is the forest primeval; but where are the hearts that beneath it
>
> Leaped like the roe, when he hears in the woodland the voice of the huntsman?
>
> Where is the thatch-roofed village, the home of Acadian farmers—

Why a Student Might Have Difficulty Comprehending This Text

Well, we can start with the word *primeval*, an adjective in the post-noun position, which means it's going to be a little hard for the unsophisticated reader to see that it is modifying *forest*, and not that *forest* is the adjective modifying *primeval*.

The next challenge would be to visualize the details of the forest, and to do that, the reader has to interpret metaphor and simile (e.g., bearded, garments, Druids, harpers hoar).

The reader has to interpret that the tone of the poem is mournful (e.g., sad, disconsolate).

Here we have the literary element of setting, and infused in the setting is going to be the theme of loss. To fully understand the poem, the reader would have to perceive that the forest primeval bodes some kind of romantic loss.

Using Literary Text in the Subject Areas

Don't overlook the importance of offering literary text in your subject area. Literary writing can deepen understandings and arouse interest in science, mathematics, languages, and social studies. Literary nonfiction is a much underused resource for extending learning, and even English teachers use it not nearly enough. By "literary nonfiction," I mean the kind of writing about a subject area that lay people as well as experts would read just to enjoy the beautiful language and fascinating ideas.

Every year, the Charles Taylor prize is awarded in Canada to an author for a work of literary nonfiction (http://www.thecharlestaylorprize.ca/home.htm). Relatively new (the Charles Taylor Prize was instituted in 2000), this prize is given in honor of the great Canadian essayist Charles Taylor. Another source for great nonfiction is the National Council of Teachers of English (NCTE) Orbis Pictus Nonfiction Award (http://www.ncte.org/elem/awards/orbispictus/123611.htm).

The literary nonfiction that I'm suggesting is not poetry or even memoir or biography, as those genres are already part of what is traditionally taught in English class. I'm talking mainly about nature and science writing, the kind of writing that English teachers usually don't offer because they are unfamiliar with it, and other content area teachers don't offer because it is not organized like an informational textbook. Science and nature reading can create a bridge between the English class and science, social studies, and math classes that illuminate understandings in both subjects.

Literary nonfiction is not science fiction, nor is it biography, polemic, or the kind of text whose purpose is to expose corruption or danger. Literary nonfiction can be a single essay, an essay collection by a single author, or an anthology. It is recognizable by the poetic qualities of the language and the author's obvious intent to engage the reader in thought for its own sake, not to promote a political or social agenda. Some of my favorite authors to bring into the classroom are, for science: Annie Dillard, Hal Borland, Diane Ackerman, Verlyn Klinkenborg, Carl Sagan, and Lewis Thomas. These writers can be classified as "nature writers," and they offer observations, speculations, and metaphors nestled in the natural world.

If we teach according to the way the brain learns, then we reach outside the artificial lines that supposedly delineate subject areas. Using literary nonfiction as a resource can establish the kind of curriculum integration that makes learning meaningful and promotes creativity.

The reader of literary nonfiction does not have to feel compelled to read the book sequentially from cover to cover like a novel. The idea is to dip in to segments that attract us. Many people feel that they are not doing the right thing with a book if they don't read all of it, but this is a false notion. Literary nonfiction makes no demands on the reader's time.

Collaborate with your library-media specialist to create displays, hold book talks to stimulate interest in particular titles, set aside classroom mini-libraries, and make students aware of literary nonfiction that would build background knowledge in your subject. One of the most powerful, memorable, durable ways to learn anything is through a story. As a teacher, you know this, because every year you accumulate stories, and you add them to your teaching repertoire because *they work*.

You can tie the literary nonfiction to an inquiry-based project, in which students use a multiplicity of sources to pursue a question. I think that the best way to do this is through a Web quest, in which the problem to be solved and the resources needed to solve it are collected on the Internet. You can create your own Web quests, or you can use one of the incredible number of excellent ones already available. I suggest doing a search on www.filamentality.com. If you aren't familiar with this resource, you're in for a pleasant surprise at what's out there, ready to go.

Finally, there are a number of wonderful readers' anthologies, such as *The Prose Reader: Essays for Thinking, Reading, and Writing* edited by Kim and Michael Flashmann, that contain superb samplings of literary nonfiction on a variety of topics. I'm sure that your students could connect to at least one of the essays in anthologies like this.

III

The Strategies

Using the Strategies

Select just *one* strategy for a segment of text. There are two ways to do this. Remember that your goal is to have students call on their strategies automatically and to internalize the strategies so that they know what to do to prepare for reading, focus on comprehension, and continue thinking and creating meaning after they close the book.

You could march through the before-reading, during-reading, and after-reading strategies in sequence, adapting them to the text. Most of the strategies are applicable to most text; some match more readily than others to certain texts. If you choose this procedure, you can choose as much time on each strategy as you deem necessary: You could run through all of them in a few weeks, and then revisit them as necessary throughout the year. Or, you could decide to spend several weeks on each one, leaving the last quarter of the school year to have the students read independently, applying what they learned about how to approach a reading task.

If you work with a team composed of teachers of various subjects, you might choose to coordinate with multiple teachers working on the same strategies while the students apply them to their various texts. Such a team effort would reinforce the message that there's more to reading than just looking like a person who is reading, and that we do have considerable control over how well we comprehend text.

5

The *Before-Reading* Strategies

Establish a Purpose for Reading

This is the before-reading strategy of establishing a purpose for reading. A key difference between successful and unsuccessful readers in school is that the former adjust their reading pace and mindset in accordance with a known purpose for reading. The latter group does not adjust pace to suit the purpose because when they approach a reading task, they don't really know what they are looking for.

Think about how purpose shapes experience in the example of shopping. It's a lovely Sunday, your weekend obligations are done, and you'd like to spend a leisurely afternoon wandering around an outlet mall about an hour's drive from your house. Taking along a friend who's out for the same kind of adventure, you go window shopping, making mental notes about things you'd like to buy when you have the money. The next day, your son informs you that he is in immediate need for hiking boots. On your way home from work, you pull in to the local Big Box store, make a beeline for the No Nonsense Footwear department, where you know exactly where to find your quarry. A few minutes at the express checkout (you get lucky, someone offers to let you go first) and you're back in your car. Obviously, we have two entirely different strategies applied to two different purposes for the activity known as shopping.

We can divide the activity known as reading into three categories based on purpose: skimming, scanning, and close reading. These three purpose can be used together on the same piece of text. I'll discuss these in terms of purpose and process.

The purpose of skimming is to get an overview, a general idea. We can think of it as a walk-through, a quick visual, of the territory. There are three good reasons to skim:

1. We want to establish a base coat of knowledge before reading carefully. This base coat will give detailed information something to stick to.

2. We want to decide if something is worth reading.

3. All we need is a general idea of the material.

Any kind of informational text can be skimmed for one of these reasons, but fiction and poetry are *not* meant to be skimmed. If we do so, we are violating the author's intent, and reading in accordance with author's intent has a lot to do with comprehension. Literary (as opposed to informational) writers have a habit of sticking extremely important, story-changing information where the reader least expects it, such as in the middle of a paragraph in the middle of a chapter with an unassuming title. Also, to skim a novel is to deny yourself the immersion in setting and character that is the whole point of reading a novel. It's exactly like fast-forwarding through a movie and then declaring that the movie did not absorb your attention.

As to the process of skimming, the best way is to let the text features do that for you: Let the visual cues on the page tell you what's important. In informational text, important information is going to be exactly where you expect it to be: beginning and endings of chapters and paragraphs.

Scanning is "looking up." The purpose of scanning is to locate specific information to answer a question. The best way to scan is to use the index or the table of contents, but you'll see a lot of inefficient readers who don't bother to do this and instead waste time flipping pages in search of a needle in a haystack. Efficient readers use cues such as bookmarks and textual notations to make scanning easier later on.

In a world where locating information is an essential, the ability to scan is increasingly important. Scanning involves the skill of knowing where to find sought-after information from the vast array of sources available in print and on the Internet. Once we find our key words, say in a Google search, we need to scan the words around it and quickly perceive the main idea and the overall tone of the document to see if it will suit our purposes. Library media specialists should be able to give lessons in scanning.

Close reading is the kind of reading that is required for reading comprehension tests and for serious and technical literature. By "serious literature," I mean literature with a meaning that is subtle, implied, and can be interpreted in more than one way. By "technical literature," I mean literature with a meaning that depends on the understanding of highly domain-specific words and phrases. In serious and technical literature, the sentences are not only lengthy but also highly complex grammatically (containing multiple phrases, clauses, and relative pronouns).

As I mentioned earlier, close reading often does begin with skimming. Skimming and scanning are strategies for close reading. Rereading is another strategy, as I'll talk about in Chapter 6.

Skillful readers are used to knowing, before they begin reading, what they are looking for. They establish expectations, and once you do that for anything, whether it be for seeing a movie, attending a social event, or reading a book or a document, you are in position to have a smooth experience. It is when our expectations are contradicted that we feel disoriented and vulnerable.

The following is a simple guide that is meant to initiate the habit of thinking about purpose and expectations before you read.

The Thinking Reader's Guide to Reading: Setting a Purpose and Establishing Expectations for Reading

What am I about to read?

Approximately how long do I plan to spend reading today?

Approximately how many pages will I read today?

What is my purpose? What am I looking for?

What are my expectations? Check off the items that apply:

Mostly new information about a new topic: _____

More about a familiar topic: _____

I will be:

    Skimming: _____ Scanning: _____ Reading closely: _____

Three questions that I expect this text to answer are:

    a. _____

    b. _____

    c. _____

If you want, you can code these questions in the following ways:

Main Idea Answer: A main idea will be repeated and stressed. It will appear throughout the chapter. It will explain itself with reasons and examples. The graphs, tables, charts, and pictures will help you understand more about it.

Detail Answer: A detail will be mentioned in only one paragraph. A detail will relate to the main idea.

Interesting Side Knowledge: Interesting side knowledge will help you understand the main idea but will not be necessary to your understanding of it. Often, interesting side knowledge is set off in a box. Often, interesting side knowledge comes in the form of an anecdote (little story).

Having Students Reflect on Their Purposes for Reading

I realize that you are not a reading teacher, but it is possible for you to have students keep a reading journal for a week, tracking their purposes for reading whatever they do read. They will find, and so will you, that they do more reading than they thought, but their purpose for reading is so natural that they don't even notice it. This reading log exercise is worth doing because it builds students' confidence as they see that there are all kinds of reading that they already do efficiently. Have them categorize their reading as skimming, scanning, or close reading.

Here are the advantages to having students do a week-long reading journal:

1. It would lead them to compare their reading volume with that of their peers.

2. It would show them the strengths that they already have so that they can use these strengths to build better reading skills.

3. It would show them the importance and omnipresence of reading in their lives.

4. It would probably show that they spend much of their reading time skimming and scanning. That would establish the difference between skimming or scanning and close reading and give you the teachable moment to explain how skimming is the introductory step to close reading.

Mini-Lesson: Mrs. Leone Establishes a Purpose for Reading

Mrs. Leone teaches 10th-grade biology. She wants her students to read information about how the heart pumps blood and she instructs her students to read the following passage:

> The heart is capable of pumping an astonishing amount of blood. If a healthy person's heart beats approximately 70 times per minute at rest, and if each side of the heart pumps approximately 70 ml of blood, then the amount of blood pumped during each minute would come to 4,900 ml per minute, which is about 5 liters. The amount of blood that each side of the heart pumps per minute is called the cardiac output. The cardiac output changes during

(Science — vertical tab)

exercise. It may rise to 25 liters per minute during strenuous exercise. A trained athlete's cardiac output may be as high as 40 liters.

The nerves of the autonomic nervous system control cardiac output. The sympathetic nerves carrying impulses to the heart raise cardiac output by raising the rate of the heartbeat and its strength. The parasympathetic nerves carrying impulses to the heart lower cardiac output by slowing the rate of heartbeat.

Mrs. Leone wants the students to see how what they understand and remember from a reading experience can depend on the purpose that they've established before reading. In a related way, if they establish no purpose for reading, then what they understand and remember may not equip them for what they need to know.

Mrs. Leone says, "When you read something in science, you have to read with a purpose. I'm going to ask you to read a passage

> Purpose for reading influences comprehension

about cardiac output, but I'm going to divide you into three groups. Group 1, you're going to read the passage because you want to find out what factors can increase or decrease cardiac output. Group 2, you're going to read to find out how the sympathetic and parasympathetic nerves affect cardiac output. And Group 3, you're going to read to find out whether it's true that an athlete's at-rest heart rate is lower than that of a nonathlete. Go."

When the students have finished reading, Mrs. Leone asks one person from each group to respond to the question that directed the group's reading (their purpose). She will ask another person from each group to talk about how the group went about reading to satisfy their purpose. Group 1 had to read the entire passage carefully because the information that they were looking for was infused throughout the passage. Group 2 had to scan for the key words, *sympathetic* and *parasympathetic*, and then read only paragraph two, but they had to read that paragraph carefully. And Group 3 had to go scouting for the words *athlete* and *at rest*.

Analysis

This is a worthwhile expenditure of class time not only because the students stand to become better readers by thinking about purpose before they read, but also because they reinforce learning on all three questions by sharing their answers after the reading.

Mini-Lesson: Mr. Habib and Asking Questions to Establish a Purpose for Reading

Mr. Habib teaches 11th-grade social studies. Much of what he wants his students to read is primary source material. At the

> Readers establish purpose by posing questions before reading

moment, he wants them to read (abridgements of) Supreme Court decisions. The legalistic language is difficult for some students to cut through, so he uses the following mini-lesson to have his students establish a purpose for reading the cases. The mini-lesson is based on having the students pose three questions before they read.

Mr. Habib wants students to research a Supreme Court case that involves students. First, he has them read the summaries of 10 landmark cases involving students (http://www.uscourts.gov/outreach/resources/landmark_studentcases. htm). Based on these summaries, he wants his students to pose their three questions that they anticipate the original language of the ruling will answer. He wants the questions to enable the students to understand the basis of the Court's decision based on Constitutional principles. Therefore, the questions must reflect this purpose.

Mr. Habib says, "All Supreme Court decisions are based on how the issues in the case match up with the rules. The rules are spelled out in the Constitution. But, if the rules were clear to everybody, we wouldn't need a Supreme Court to play referee. That is why the Justices explain their ruling carefully. They explain how their decision comports with the way they think the Justices should be interpreting the Constitution. That is what we mean when we say that they rule on the basis of Constitutionality.

"So when you read an opinion, you have to read it from the Constitution's point of view. But the Constitution cannot talk, any more than it talks by just saying what it says. The Justices' job is to talk for the Constitution.

"After you read the summaries, the meat and potatoes of the case will be clear to you. That is when you set yourself up for reading the actual opinion by asking three questions that you expect the Justice writing the opinion will answer. But remember, your three questions should reflect the fact that the Justice is interpreting the Constitution as it relates to the case."

Analysis

Mr. Habib's mini-lesson develops critical thinking skills. The untrained student would read the Supreme Court opinion from his or own perspective, not understanding that the Justice is writing from a very particular point of view, that of the Constitution. There are many adults who can't distinguish their *own* opinions from legal opinions rendered against criteria, such as laws.

The mini-lesson also develops in the student the productive habit of thinking and focusing before reading: thinking about the perspective of the writer and the purpose of the text. The reader has a purpose for reading the text, but the text also has a purpose, one that was determined by the writer. It is when the reader and the writer understand each other's purposes that communication (comprehension) is achieved.

Summary:
Establishing a Purpose for Reading

When you first start talking to students about establishing a purpose for reading, they are likely to respond with puzzlement. What could possibly be a purpose for reading other than "just reading," they may ask. "You read because you read," they may think. "I read to get my homework done," they may say. But if you get them thinking about all the different kinds of reading, casual and formal, that they do throughout the day, they may begin to understand that all reading is not the same, nor is all reading done at the same pace, or with the same intensity.

Here are some purposes for reading:

- Find out specific information
- Verify or disprove a belief or hunch
- Define a term
- Make a comparison
- Get a general overview
- Read a different version or a different point of view about information that you already know something about
- See if there's anything new in the text on a subject that you already know a substantial amount about
- Enjoy the beauty and power of the language
- Inform a personal or business decision that you are about to make
- Be able to engage in social or professional conversation on the topic
- Enjoy the affirmation of someone who agrees with your point of view
- Derive an emotional response, such as laughter, empathy, joy, outrage, and so forth
- Follow directions so that you can do a procedure
- Clarify something that you feel you don't understand
- Review information for an upcoming test
- Satisfy curiosity
- Pass the time
- Experience something vicariously
- Take your mind off something else
- Understand the writer's perspective
- Improve your reading ability

Before Strategy: Preview
to Determine Importance and Establish Expectations

This is the before-reading strategy of previewing to determine importance and establish expectations. This strategy connects to bringing prior knowledge forward in that it prepares the mind to receive the new information. The previewing strategies lay a base coat of information to which the fully developed information can adhere. Without this base coat, the main ideas and details are likely to slide right off.

In real-life reading, we use previewing strategies all the time. Although it's said that you can't judge a book by its cover, that maxim refers to the quality of the book, whether or not you will like it. The cover does, of course, give a preview as to the book's genre, its general mood, and its intended audience. When you browse through the shelves at a bookstore, you indeed examine the book's façade, not only its cover, but also the blurb inside the jacket, the quotations touting the book, and the other titles by the same author. You are likely to thumb through the book, tasting samples of its language. When you finally start reading in earnest, you've set yourself up for a certain kind of reading experience.

The following four textual features help us preview the reading to determine importance and establish expectations:

1. Graphic information and art

2. Typographical features that direct the reader's attention

3. Summary information

4. Placement of main ideas within text

The reader should use these four textual features to preview a reading assignment in a textbook that is heavy with new information. After reading the chapter title and placing it in its context in the table of contents, the reader leafs through the pages of the target chapter, getting a feel for how long it will probably take to read it. Then, the reader peruses each map, chart, graph, table, and photograph for the purpose of establishing main ideas. After all, the editors of the textbook went to great lengths—time and expense in procuring permissions—to display these visuals. Why would they have done so except to clarify the main points?

Next, the reader reads all of the headings and subheadings. These actually form an outline of the chapter, setting forth a skeleton of its main and supportive ideas. You might even direct the students to create an outline out of the headings and subheadings, or turn them into questions. The reader would then know exactly what to expect and what to look for in the text.

After these main ideas have been established, the reader can look for summary information in the expected places, such as chapter highlights on the opening page of each chapter or end-of-chapter questions.

Moving beyond the major signposts and into text itself, opening and closing paragraphs within each main heading will usually frame the details with topic sentences.

By now, the reader has a pretty good mental closet into which the details can be placed.

Textbooks as Inauthentic Text

The preceding procedure for determining importance and establishing expectations will work only for textbooks. Textbooks, unlike novels or historical documents, are written for students. They are strong on organization, short on passion.

Authentic text, text that is written for an audience other than students, does not behave as predictably as a textbook does. You won't be able to rely on topic sentences, summary statements, and other cues quite so much.

Where does important information hide out? How does information let you know that it is important and not secondary? For one thing, important information jumps out at you in the form of typographical features that the editors have set up for your benefit.

The Thinking Reader's Guide to Reading: Previewing

What is the title of what you are about to read?

Look at the subtitles. What key words are mentioned more than once?

Describe one of the pictures.

Tell what question is answered by one of the graphs, tables, or charts.

Are there end-of-chapter questions?

What special text effects are used in this segment to get you to notice what is important?

Previewing for Unfamiliar Vocabulary

Students can come to school with a rich vocabulary in social language. However, the language that they need for school is expressed in a different register. *Register* is a term used by linguists to refer to the style of a particular speech community. By *style* we mean a level of formality or informality, specificity or looseness, of the word choices and sentence structure choices.

We don't have to be afraid of students' encountering new words in their reading. Encountering new words is how we learn them in the first place. If we have little children, we don't teach them new words. They learn new words because they've heard them used, and then they use new words because they have a need for them.

"Doing a vocabulary lesson" where the teacher defines "new words from the chapter" on the board is not, as it turns out, particularly helpful in improving reading comprehension (Nagy, 1988, p. 2). A more effective way to teach vocabulary in a way that improves reading comprehension is to limit the number of new words that are explicitly taught, but teach those words as keys to clusters of other words that are related to them.

Vocabulary education that improves reading comprehension has three features:

1. Repetition of the word in its various forms and contexts

2. Meaningful use by both the teacher and the student

3. In-depth exploration of a limited number of words that lead to the understanding of more words that have common structure (prefixes or roots), can be used to talk about a common subject (proximity of use), and have a similar meaning or opposite meaning to the target word

It is not possible, nor would it be worthwhile, to define every word that we anticipate to be unfamiliar in a given landscape of text that the students are about to read. Such an attempt would be shallow, and shallow vocabulary teaching is not a worthwhile expenditure of class time. Anyway, reading *all by itself* is what improves vocabulary in the register of the text, just as social communication, rather than looking up words in the dictionary and writing their definitions, is what improves vocabulary in the social register.

You may be saying, "But if I don't teach them the unfamiliar words before they read, they might get discouraged at all the words they don't know and give up. How can they understand if they don't understand the words?" The answer is that language, both written and spoken, offers a lot of context clues and built-in redundancies that allow us to derive meaning of the whole without understanding every one of the words. The answer, also, lies in judicious selection of words in a text that we will teach explicitly, as a previewing strategy.

One way to do this is to have the students pick out a few (just a few) words that they don't know in text that is facing them. The first thing they need to do is see if they can figure out what the words mean using context clues. If they can't, then they need to ask themselves if the words that they have in mind appear multiple times in the text. If they do, and they can't be figured out by context clues, then those words are good candidates for a full-on lesson.

A second way is for teachers to determine what words are needed to name new concepts, not just new labels for familiar things. Those are the words (and phrases) to go after in a big way. A good previewing strategy is to identify the key words, words that knock on our doors not because we already know what they mean and how they are in costume, but those that are actually needed to name an idea that is being explained in the chapter.

Obviously, what I'm asking is that teachers and students think critically about unfamiliar words, asking these questions:

♦ Is this a word that I can't figure out through context?

♦ Is this a word that is necessary to my understanding of the whole, or is this a word that I can let slide for now?

♦ Is this a word that is repeated?

♦ Is this a word that bears a specific meaning in this subject area?

♦ Is it a phrase, rather than a single word, that I need to learn?

♦ Is this a familiar word used in an unfamiliar way?

So, certainly, scanning for unfamiliar vocabulary, especially for words that are bold-faced to bring attention to their newness and importance, is a previewing strategy. But to bombard students with a list of every single word that may be unfamiliar to them is not as effective as selecting just a few words and teaching them in depth and as keys to learning other words.

Previewing by Using Textual Features to Distinguish Main Ideas from Supportive Information and Details

Mini-Lesson: Three levels of Importance: Critical, Important, Nice to Know

Reading comprehension depends on the reader's ability to foreground the main ideas. Readers need to determine what are the most important ideas in the text, and we will designate those as **critical.** We will designate the supportive ideas as **important,** and the details as **nice to know.** The visual features in a textbook will give you strong cues as to what is critical, what is important, what is just nice to know.

Social Studies

Mini-Lesson:
Mr. Wolfe and Determining Levels of Importance in Social Studies

 Example: Social Studies Textbook

From *Enjoying American History.*

> Between 1870 and 1890, about 10 million settlers moved west of the Mississippi River. Many went to claim free land. Congress, responding to pressure from Westerners, passed the Homestead Act in 1862. It provided that any adult male citizen could acquire a 160-acre farm on public land simply by paying a registration fee and staying on the farm for five years. To get title more quickly, a homesteader could buy the land for $125 an acre.
>
> In addition, the federal government gave 131 million acres to the railroads and 140 million acres to the states during the period from 1870 to 1890. Most of this land was sold or given away to land-hungry settlers. In this way the railroads were assured new customers and the states acquired new settlers.

Why a Student Might Have Difficulty Comprehending This Text

The key to extracting meaning from text like this for the purpose of learning history is to set up a mental hierarchy about what is the most and the least important. Mr. Wolfe knows that, left to their own devices, his eighth grade students will highlight far too much of the text for their highlightings to be useful. Therefore, he gives the following before-reading mini-lesson on color-coding to determine importance.

Use highlighting judiciously (rather than highlighting almost everything)

Mr. Wolfe says, "You know how, when I ask you to highlight important information, you end up highlighting the whole thing? I understand why you're doing that, but if you highlight everything, then you might as well not highlight anything because nothing stands out. So let's try it a different way. I'm giving you a page about Westward Expansion, and I want you to highlight it, but this time, we're going to do the reverse. Instead of highlighting what you think is the most important, first highlight the details that you think are the *least important.* That could be a whole sentence, or a phrase here and there. Then, with a different color, highlight information that you think is *important, but not the most important.* And after you've done that, take a third color, and what you have left should be the most important, the *critical* information.

"After you're finished highlighting, your paper will be very colorful. I want you to then set up three columns and write notes—not whole sentences, just notes—for each column. We're calling the first column, critical information; we're calling the second, important information, and we're calling the third, nice to know."

Analysis

You can see how Mr. Wolfe has worked with something that the students were used to doing, highlighting, but doing imperfectly. His two-phase activity for the students has note-taking building on reading. The lesson is accessible to the students, gives them a purpose for reading and a postreading wrap-up, and teaches the skill of distinguishing levels of importance in text.

Here's another social studies reading Mr. Wolfe gave his eighth-grade students:

> In effect, what the leaders agreed on at Camp David was only a framework for peace. Final details still had to be added. Israeli and Egyptian officials worked for several more months before a peace treaty was signed in March, 1979.

> Egypt became the first Arab nation to open diplomatic relations with Israel. Israel gave back the rest of the Sinai Peninsula, with a peacekeeping force from other nations in the eastern Sinai serving as a buffer between Israeli and Egyptian troops. Israel agreed to enter negotiations on the future of the West Bank and the Gaza Strip.

Mr. Wolfe says, "This is a very short piece, but it answers a lot of questions. Not all of the questions are of equal importance. On your | Use student-generated questions as a focus for comprehension
paper, I want you to write three questions that are answered in this piece. Don't write the answers, just the questions. (If you can write the questions, then I know you can find the answers.) Although, there is one thing: Write the questions in size order, with the most critical first and in the largest letters, the important second and in medium letters, and the nice-to-know third and in the smallest letters, but still readable."

Analysis

Mr. Wolfe has varied the way he has students process levels of importance, but he continues to have students focus on this essential reading comprehension skill. If you try to do this exercise yourself, you might find it to be quite challenging, engaging, and informative.

Mini-Lesson:
Mrs. Loftus Examines Visual Patterns in a Latin Textbook

The focus of this mini-lesson is that visual patterns in the text are there to set up mental patterns for grammatical rules in the target language. If students consciously accept the visual structures (charts) that show the grammar, they stand a much better chance of remembering and applying the rules than if they treat the chart as ordinary text, rather than as a pattern.

 Example: Foreign Language Textbook

Verbs

Verbs tell what a subject does, has, or is. The verb resides in the predicate, along with the modifiers of the verb, if there are any.

Puella parva *est.*   The girl *is* small. (part)
Puellae *laborant.*   The girls *work.* (whole)

In addition to expressing action, ownership, or state of being, verbs also tell whether the action (ownership or state of being) is in the past, present, or future. This time-telling function of the verb is known as *tense.* One difference between English and Latin is that not every single English verb changes its ending to show tense, but every single Latin verb does change its ending to show tense.

Videō	*I see*		Vidī	*I saw*
Audiō	*I hear*		Audivī	*I heard*
Ponō	*I put*		Posuī	*I put*

We speak of verbs as having three *persons* in both the singular and the plural. In English we indicate the persons by using personal pronouns, as follows. (The personal pronouns that follow are in the *subjective case*, and we will explain that later on.)

Person	*Singular*	*Plural*
First (the person speaking)	I	we
Second (the person spoken to)	you	you
Third (the person or thing spoken about)	he, she, it	they

In English, we include the personal pronoun, but in Latin, we generally omit it. The information that the personal pronoun would show (person, number, gender) is shown in Latin by the verb ending alone. Here are the most common Latin verb endings for persons:

Singular		*Plural*	
I	-ō (or –*m*)	we	-*mus*
You	-*s*	you	-*tis*
He, she, it	-*t*	they	-*nt*

Because in Latin you will not have the personal pronouns to tell you person, number, and gender, you must become familiar with these endings and what they signify.

Where a Student Might Have Difficulty Comprehending This Text

This text requires the reader to absorb information through charts rather than through paragraphs. Charted information is visually appealing and inviting to the reader because white space on the page is usually a welcome respite from density of text. However, charted information is, by definition, piecemeal. Bits of information not anchored by sentences can be hard to comprehend because the reader can't link it to a larger meaning.

Foreign language reading has a lot of charted information like this, where the reader is expected to absorb information that is unconnected to a meaningful sentence and is offered for memorization. The challenge is not only the unconnected nature of the information, but the fact that the sounds themselves are meaningless, or just starting to take on meaning, for the reader.

Mini-Lesson: Mrs. Loftus on Visual Patterns

Mrs. Loftus says, "Let's start today with a mini-lesson on how to use the visuals in the text to help us understand and remember the infor-

> Take meaning cues from text visuals and text layout

mation. Without opening the textbook, picture a page from it. What do you see?"

The students say things such as: columns, pictures of Rome, boxes with bits of special information that's supposed to be interesting, cartoons of guys on chariots, pictures of guys wearing togas, and so on.

Mrs. Loftus says, "Is there a lot of white space on the pages?"

The students say that, yes, there is.

Mrs. Loftus says, "Why do you think there's so much white space on the pages? If you were making a textbook, wouldn't that be more expensive? To have all that white space?"

The students shrug. They've never thought about why the publisher would be wasting so much usable space. One student says, "Maybe they just want to make a fatter book so it will cost more to buy."

Mrs. Loftus smiles. "Maybe. But maybe, the white space is there so that you'll pay more attention to the Latin words. Kind of like giving them room to breathe on the page? Let's look at a page that has a lot of white space." She gives the students time to open their books. Most open to a page that displays words in chart form.

"Most of us are looking at a page that has a chart. What does the chart show?" The students respond that, obviously, the chart shows the forms of a word class in Latin and how the endings display "something about grammar."

Mrs. Loftus points out that the chart is displaying a pattern and is doing everything that the editors can do with visuals to imprint the pattern in the mind of the reader. "The editors want your brain to take a picture of this chart. That's why they give it to you in a pattern. They don't expect your brain to take a picture of the information that is in paragraphs."

A student says, "But we don't have a photographic memory."

Mrs. Loftus says, "It would be rare to have a photographic memory for a whole paragraph, or even a sentence. That is not the way the brain remembers information. But with a chart, it's different. With a chart, you can take a mental picture of just the outlines of the chart itself, not necessarily the specific words in the chart. Your brain can accept the pattern. Language is all about patterns. That is why a good language textbook will help you by setting up the patterns in a chart. It's like giving you a toolbox or a jewelry box that has compartments in it. Who has a jewelry box or a toolbox at home?"

Many students respond that they do. One student says: "Does a shoebox count?"

"Where's the shoebox?"

"In my closet."

Mrs. Loftus smiles. "Count the shoebox as a compartment in the closet then."

Mrs. Loftus gets the students to recognize the relationship between organization and memory by pointing out the mental ability to remember that which is organized. "A toolbox, or a jewelry box or a closet is like a graphic organizer in real life. I bet that if you picture that organizer, you can see in your mind's eye were everything is inside it. Maybe not everything, but can you picture where some things are?" The students respond that, yes, they can see the contents of the box or closet.

"The charts on the page work like that. If you have a pattern, it works like a box or a cabinet with shelves and compartments in your brain. And that organizer helps your brain remember things. When we learned our first language, and for most of us that was English or Spanish, we didn't learn by looking at charts. We learned by setting up mental charts based on the language that we heard and our mind's remarkable ability to learn language. But we don't hear Latin spoken enough to set up those mental charts. That's why we have these charts on paper.

"What would be one sentence that summarizes what we've been talking about? Write a summary sentence in your Reading Latin notes.

Mrs. Loftus is looking for a summary sentence that expresses the importance of connecting charted information to mental patterns that are essential to learning the grammar of a new language.

"I hope you have the words 'charts,' 'patterns,' and 'remember,' or words to that effect, in your summary sentence."

Analysis

Mrs. Loftus's mini-lesson capitalizes on the brain's natural organizing ability. She's also made the connection between the Latin textbook and familiar items that the students have at home to store things. The mini-lesson opens students' minds to using the textbook layout as an organizing tool.

Mini-Lesson:
Ms. Ortiz Uses Textual Features to Preview Math Text

Glance through a mathematics text. You will find all kinds of special features on every page:

> Take meaning cues from text visuals and text layout

- Headings
- Boxed information to draw attention to rules and principles
- Tables
- Bold-faced print to draw attention to new terminology (single words and phrases)
- Numbered lists
- Annotated math problems
- Marginal notes giving directions for doing a procedure
- Highlighted boxes for problem-solving tips
- Arrows
- Examples
- Anecdotal information explaining modern and historical applications of a particular mathematical principal accompanied by a photograph
- Mathematical symbols
- Graphs
- Blueprints
- Pie charts

- Geometric shapes, sides and angles labeled
- Blank spaces indicating where the answers should go on a separate sheet of paper
- Maps of roadways
- Maps and photographs of geographic features

All of these images must be *read*. That is to say, meaning must be extracted from them. The layout on the page is a clue to how meaning is to be extracted. This is a very different kind of reading experience from what the student receives reading instruction in. When required to read math, many students feel lost on the page. They don't have a systematic way of approaching the variety of information presented on a math page.

Nina Ortiz teaches math to seventh- and eighth-grade students. Here's her mini-lesson on how to use the textual features to extract meaning from a math page:

Ms. Ortiz says, "Let's talk about what a math page actually looks like. Turn to pages 466 and 467. These pages are in our chapter topic on absolute value equations. Let's make a list of every kind of print or picture that we see on these two pages." Ms. Ortiz writes the students' responses on the board, compiling a list much like the one preceding.

"Let's talk about colors now. The text isn't written in black and white. We have lots of colors. Some of the colors are used just to show you how the math we're learning is connected to the real world that we live in, like the color photographs. And some of the colors are there to show the titles of the segments because the titles are the main ideas. But, some of the colors are there to teach you math. For example, look at the red arrows inside the graph in the lower left corner. Do you see how those arrows are showing you where to look so that the solution makes sense?"

As with any kind of specialized text, the reader has to learn how to approach the page, where to look first, what to pay attention to, what to ignore. In their zest to enliven math textbooks, publishers have gone to great expense and effort to include photographs. The photographs are supposed to make real world connections to the mathematical concepts. Therefore, these photographs are informational, and if you explain why they appear, you could be illuminating a mathematical concept or at least motivating the students to consider abstract mathematical ideas relevant to and present in their lives.

Ms. Ortiz wants her students to be oriented toward meaning when they look at a math page. She says, "Here are five questions I want you to ask yourself when you open your math text to do your homework, when you study, or when you catch up on what you missed when you were absent:

"One: Is this the page showing me the heading of this chapter segment? If so, I need to take a breather to remember what I know about this topic. If not, I need to turn back until I get the heading for this chapter segment. I need to know my key idea.

"Two: Are there principles and rules on this page? If there are, they are probably set off in a box or an oval. I need to read that. If there are any words or phrases that I don't know, I need to find their definitions.

"Three: If they are new definitions, I need to look for them in bold-faced print on that page or a previous page.

"Four: If there are any graphs or tables, I need to look at them now and use the nearby words to find out what those graphs or tables mean.

"Five: Is there a photograph? I should know how this photograph is showing me how the math connects to real life.

"Once you've asked these five questions, you'll be ready to do the problems or read the explanations. But you've got to take the intelligent approach to the page. That page is trying its hardest to help you understand the math. So don't ignore the road signs on the page. Let them guide you."

Analysis

Ms. Ortiz's simple mini-lesson about using the textual features to extract meaning from a math page establishes that important *entrance foyer* that learners need to figure out where they are and what's important there. This is a skill that will help them read blueprints, maps, Web sites, magazines, and newspapers.

More on Using Textual Features to Read Math

Math readers need to be able to interpret data that is presented through a visual organizer such as a graph or chart. The graph or chart is an abstraction, a map of sorts. As with any kind of map reading, the skill of interpreting graphs and charts improves with practice. The first step is to understand exactly what information is displayed on the graph or chart. Then, the reader needs orientation: knowledge about where to begin looking at the graph or chart. This kind of skill-building is sometimes called *whole-part-whole.* That means the reader gets the gist, the meaning of the graph or chart (whole). Then, the reader examines the itemized information (part). And then, the reader draws conclusions about the itemized information (whole). Whole-part-whole thinking is an important skill for making sense of an abstract representation. Students who have difficulty making sense of graphs and charts will often say, "I don't know where to begin" when asked to explain their response to the task. They are intimidated by the lines and boxes, not understanding what they mean. The whole-part-whole sequence demystifies the information in the graph or chart.

Ms. Ortiz says, "The first thing you need to know about a graph or chart is what question it is answering. If there's a caption, read it. If there's a title, read it. If there's an introduction, read it. Then ask yourself: What question is this graph, table, or chart answering?

"Step two is to read the legend or key and the words along the X and Y axes. Step three: Now you're ready to use the graph, table, or chart to answer the question. Look for trends: What is increasing? What is decreasing? What is frequent? What is infrequent? Where are the extremes, and what do they mean? Step four: Now you want to draw conclusions that you can state in your own words."

Activating Prior Knowledge

This is the before-reading strategy of using (activating) prior knowledge to make meaning out of text. The words "prior knowledge" are never far from the words "reading comprehension." That it becomes easier to comprehend that which you already know a lot about seems too obvious to mention. But if we think of reading comprehension as the process of adding new information to known information, we begin to understand the significance of activating, or gathering, prior knowledge to face a reading task.

The fact is, a great deal of text contains information that the writer *expects* the reader to be familiar with. This expectation manifests in the writer's vocabulary choices, the number of abstract concepts, domain-specific uses of words, the amount of explanation that is supplied, and other assumptions that the writer makes about the reader's *ability* to comprehend the text based on nothing other than prior knowledge.

Every writer writes for an audience and in so doing, makes assumptions about what the audience knows and what they need to have explained. If the reader's prior knowledge about the subject falls short of the writer's assumptions about what the reader brings to the text, comprehension will fall short of the writer's expectations. If you want a taste of what I'm talking about, pick up the editorial page of a sophisticated newspaper and read an editorial about something you know little about. Now read a neighboring editorial about something that you do know something about. Note the difference in effort that is called for in comprehending the former. Take a close look at that editorial that is about a familiar subject. Consider just how much of the text you can glance over very rapidly without cost to comprehension.

Reading is a process-based activity, but processing strategies alone will not make up for a lack of knowledge of facts and knowledge about language (vocabulary and syntax). Knowledge of facts and language constitutes the capital that we bring to the investment of reading. To extend that metaphor, think of prior knowledge of facts and language as the money that a would-be investor would bring to a financial transaction. Certainly, that investor needs to have strategy, needs to know how to comparison shop, how to strike a good bargain, but his or her limits will be defined largely by his or her bank account. Strategies alone won't help in the short run, although in the long run, strategies will—should—get him or her more money so that he or she can invest better in the future.

It is not a strategy to build prior knowledge: That is done in the course of living and learning. Building prior knowledge about your subject is what you do *mainly*, when you're not "teaching reading." The strategy, however, is teaching students ways to activate prior knowledge (some of which you've already taught them, some of which they've learned in school, some of which they've learned from life experience) and use it to unlock meaning in text containing more information about something that they already know about.

My favorite strategy for activating prior knowledge, the one that I think is most authentic and appropriate for secondary students, is a form of verbal brainstorming. Ask the students to form trios and exchange what they know about the topic about which they are about to read. This brainstorming should take three minutes, no more, lest the conversations stray. Then, tell the class some of the words and ideas that you heard as you listened to the buzz. I call this the *buzz-back.*

Prior knowledge does not have to be literal. We can understand something because its paradigm, its *model,* is similar to something that we know. One of the most welcome comments we can hear our students say is, "Oh, I get it. It's like…" Student who say this are trying to find a place in their brain closets where the new information belongs. Educational psychologists call the brain's closet by the esoteric word *schemata,* with the plural being *schema.* Schema can be any kind of system for knowledge storage that the brain has already set up in which to understand something else. It is having schema that allows us to make sense of new information, to organize it, to find a pattern that allows prediction, inference, and evaluation.

The way readers decide to use prior knowledge efficiently will depend on their purpose for reading because not all prior knowledge is relevant. In Billmeyer and Barton's guide *Teaching Reading in the Content Areas: If Not Me, Who?*, they give this example: "…students told to read a description of a house as if they were home buyers were able to recall the location and number of bathrooms, whereas students who were told to read the passage from the perspective of a burglar remembered information about security systems and the number and location of windows (1998, p. 63). Graphic organizers can help students access prior knowledge.

Prior Knowledge of Vocabulary

As you would expect, readers need to apply prior knowledge to unfamiliar vocabulary. Knowledge about what a word means comes to us bit by bit after multiple exposures to the word. Each time we encounter a word in context, its context supplies a bit more information until we finally know that word well enough to use it ourselves or treat it as just another word capable of supplying meaning to yet new words.

Consider the different kinds of text and the new vocabulary that we encounter in them. Explanatory text has controlled vocabulary. This is the kind of language that we find in a textbook. The writers of the textbook are aware that they are speaking to a novice. They feed the novice/reader new information in a deliberate manner, sentence by sentence. The new vocabulary lives in a controlled environment, with generous, domain-specific definitions that are easily accessible. The new words are made visually prominent and can be delivered with examples and even pictures.

Primary sources often contain unfamiliar vocabulary. Primary sources can present copious new vocabulary without explanation or strong context clues. Primary sources can be public information such as speeches, laws, proclamations; they can be private correspondence such as personal letters or diaries; they can be literary, such as poetry.

You can see how the vocabulary of primary documents could pose a serious vocabulary challenge. To use prior knowledge of vocabulary, the reader would have to think about the kind of language that might appear in these genres. For example, in public documents, the vocabulary consists of polysyllabic words used in legal language, and these are accessible through our knowledge of word components.

In private correspondence, we can find unfamiliar nouns (for things that existed in the world of the writer, but not in ours), and we can use our knowledge of the world of the writer to access these. For example, in a soldier's letter, we could expect to find words for military supplies. In poetry, we can expect to find words that carry metaphorical meaning. We can access these meanings with prior knowledge of connotation.

Knowledge Building: Three Models

Let's think of using background knowledge as forming three kinds of learning models: accumulation, refining, and reconstructing. In the first, accumulation, you have a strong and valid structure, a basic understanding that does not need to change for you to add information accumulated from additional input. In refining knowledge, we make minor adjustments to correct misunderstandings. In the reconstruction model, we need to throw out structures and information that we find are no longer valid. This last is the most difficult to do because we don't want to disregard beliefs that we thought were facts. For example, you may admire a person or institution and receive information that would undermine your assumptions were you to accept it into your schema. It can take repeated exposures to that contradictory information or additional assaults to your beliefs before you are willing to reconstruct your knowledge of it. One way of understanding this is that we are always trying to fit new information into an old box, and it takes a while before we admit that the old box isn't going to work, and we need to construct a whole new box. Understandings of science, economics, education, and other complex systems require reconstruction of knowledge (and we've seen the resistance to the paradigm changes often enough).

Mini-Lessons for Building and Using Prior Knowledge

The most well-known model for building and using prior knowledge is the KWL (what I know, what I want to know, what I have learned) chart, and it's certainly an effective strategy, but older students may feel condescended to if you try to get them to use it, so we need to find more sophisticated versions of the KWL model.

Mini-Lesson:
English, Mrs. Barth's Stealth KWL and Word Sort

Mrs. Barth is an eighth-grade English teacher. She is teaching her students about the different varieties of the English language, and she has gathered together a lot of readings for

An advancement of the KWL chart that is appropriate for secondary level students

them. One of these is called "Village English in Rural Alaska" by Hannah Paniyavluk Loon. She writes the following list (see Figure 5.1) on the board and asks the students to make three columns: words/phrases that they know on the left; words/phrases that they don't know on the right; not sure in the center.

Figure 5.1. KLW Chart

Inupiaq	*Intergroup Communication*	*Village English*
Northwest Alaska	Standard English	Naluagmiu

This sorting sparks a bit of interesting conversation that serves as the introduction to the short article. Mrs. Barth has succeeded in having the students write a KWL chart without even knowing that that is what they were doing.

Mini-Lesson: Earth Science,
Mrs. Ziegler's Rocks, Classification, and Ice Cream

"Okay, this week your reading is going to be about how different kinds of rocks are classified. You will be reading about how rocks are classified into three major categories: igneous, sedimentary, and metamorphic. You'll be reading about what those three kinds of rocks look like and how they were formed.

"This week's reading strategy is called *activating prior knowledge.* When you read in science, you're introducing new information to your brain. You can't just throw it in there like it's a pair of socks that you're shoving into a drawer. Information enters your brain by making friends with other information that is already there. If you don't, then the new information will think it wandered into a place where it doesn't know anybody, and it will leave. You want that new information to feel welcome.

Making new information feel like it has friends in your brain is what we mean by activating prior knowledge.

"So, let's do that. I told you that we'll be reading about the different kinds of rocks and what they are called. I want you to think about two things. The first, and you probably knew I was going to say this, is rocks. On a page of your notebook, write the word *rock* right in the middle of the page. Let's do a two-minute brainstorm and write what we know about the rocks of the earth. Work with a partner.

"Now we've thought about rocks. What else? Well, I want you to think about classifications. We do that a lot in science. Think about how things are organized, classified into groups of like features. Think about ice cream. How can ice cream be classified?"

The students come up with different kinds of classification systems: by flavor, by brand, by fat content, by texture. "It doesn't matter what kind of classification system you have," Mrs. Zeigler says. "But I want you to set up a chart for how you would show someone how your ice cream classification system works."

Analysis

Mrs. Zeigler has capitalized on two kinds of learning: facts and systems. The students do have prior knowledge about the subject, rocks, but they are going to be looking at this subject in a scientific way. Rather than having them think that what they already know is irrelevant to a scientific understanding of rocks and classification systems, she's made them feel that they are ready to add to existing knowledge and can trust their experience while being open to new perspectives.

Mini-Lesson:
Latin, Mr. Patel and Language 1 to Language 2

"The reading strategy that we're learning to do this week is called *activating prior knowledge.* What that means in Latin class is that even though you don't speak Latin, you can use what you know about English to understand how Latin works. When we grow up speaking our native language, we learn rules, but we don't even know we're learning them. Somewhere along the line, you've learned that in English you can use the order of the words in the sentence to signify the relationship of those words to each other. You know that *Everybody loves Raymond* means one thing and *Raymond loves everybody* means another. That is because English is what we call a *word-order* language. That's a rule that you learned unconsciously, but you know perfectly well how to use it. Well, when we learn another language, we have to learn the rules consciously because we are coming to it as outsiders. Latin is not a word-order language. It's a language that uses inflections (endings) to indicate what in English is indicated by word order: how words relate to each other in the sentence. To get to the new language, to get it to make sense to you, you first have to realize how much you already know about language rules and your ability to learn them. We call that *using language I to learn language II.*

"We're about to read about how nouns and pronouns in Latin operate differently from nouns and pronouns in English. You know how pronouns in English can be masculine or feminine, as in he, him; she, her? From each of these pronouns in English, we can determine whether it is masculine or feminine, whether it is subjective or objective (where it belongs in the sentence) and whether it is singular or plural. Well, what we're going to be reading about is how in Latin, all nouns, not only pronouns, are capable of telling us those three bits of information: gender, case, and number."

 ## Example: Foreign Language Textbook

Gender

In English we are used to the term *gender* referring to a living being that is either male or female. We say *father, uncle, brother, master, stallion, actor*, and *he* for masculine beings; *mother, aunt, sister, mistress, mare, actress*, and *she* for feminine beings. Latin is like English in that Latin makes distinctions between masculine and feminine living beings. However, Latin does something with gender that English does not do: Latin assigns gender for nonliving things as well. In English, nonliving things are considered neuter, that is, having neither a male or a female gender.

It will probably surprise you to know that Latin and the languages closely derived from it (Spanish, French, Portuguese, Italian, and Romanian) consider nonliving things to be masculine or feminine, and they have masculine or feminine endings to denote gender not only for nouns, but also for the adjectives that modify them. Thus, the word *via* (i.e., *way*, in English) is feminine, having a feminine ending; *carrus* (i.e., *cart*, in English) is masculine, having a masculine ending. We call the concept of naming a nonliving thing as masculine or feminine *grammatical gender*. Grammatical gender does not have to do with the meaning of the word. There's nothing feminine or masculine inherently about the words *via* and *carrus*.

Nouns of the first declension use the *-a* ending to indicate that they are feminine. (There are a few nouns of the first declension that name males specifically, and these are masculine, taking the masculine ending *-us*). Nouns of the second declension ending in *-us* are masculine. Other nouns in the second declension that end in *-um* are neuter when they are regular. The nouns of the first and second declension obey these rules. However, the nouns of the other declensions do not obey rules and therefore must be memorized individually.

Why a Student Might Have Difficulty Comprehending This Text

The term *declension,* a key term in this text, is used only in Latin class for the students. Not only do the native speakers of English not use the term declension, they don't use the concept (of inflecting nouns as declensions) either. So, the key term is not only a foreign word, it is a foreign *notion.* Furthermore, the text is referring to first, second, and other declensions, taking an unfamiliar concept to even more unfamiliar territory.

When in unfamiliar territory, we take out our maps to see what we can recognize to get our bearings. So it is with reading comprehension, or when learning any new subject. Students will be in a better position to understand this text on grammatical gender if they understand the gender concept in English words. Have them add to the list of nouns in English that connote gender, and then have them list nongendered nouns in English and compare that list to the gendered nouns in the target language. The more they bring what they know to the conscious level, the more they can absorb (related) new information.

The issue of gender in a foreign language would not, of course, be introduced by having the students read the textbook. The textbook information is supportive, to be used for clarification and review.

The Genitive Case

In English, the objective case following the preposition *of* shows various relationships between nouns, including the idea of possession or ownership. (There is also a possessive case in English indicated by the addition of -*'s,* or -*s',* or sometimes by the apostrophe alone, to the word indicating the owner.)

In Latin, these various relations between nouns are expressed by endings in the genitive case. No separate word meaning *of* or punctuation mark such as the apostrophe is needed.

Latin expresses the relationship of possessor and possessed (two nouns) by attaching the genitive case ending to the word indicating the possessor. The endings of the genitive case for nouns and adjectives of the first and second declension are as follows:

	Singular	*Plural*
First Declension	**-ae** -viae *roads* *of the roads*	**-ārum** -viārum *roads';* *of the roads*
Second Declension	**-i** -serv *slave's;* *of (the) slave*	**-ōrum** servōrum *slaves';* *of (the) slaves*

Analysis

Activating prior knowledge about language is always a key teaching strategy for teaching another language. Here, Mr. Patel has extended that strategy to reading comprehension so that students can stay grounded as they read.

The following are other mini-lessons that activate prior knowledge as a before-reading strategy:

- ◆ KWL charts and their variations have students establish what they already know, what they would like to know, and then after reading, what they learned by reading

- ◆ Discussions.

- ◆ Think-pair-share.

- ◆ Graphic organizers.

- ◆ Word banks.

- ◆ ABC brainstorm: In this activity, students try to think of one word that they know about the topic matched to each letter of the alphabet. Variations would be to think of one word that they know matched to each letter of their names, the name of the school, the name of their favorite athlete or team, and so on.

- ◆ Semantic mapping: This is a cross between the free thinking of brainstorming and the visual organization of a graphic organizer. A semantic map is a cluster diagram representing the set of words and their forms that are related to a topic.

- ◆ Pictures that evoke associations about the topic.

- ◆ Evocation of personal experience.

Finally, don't forget about the role played by metaphor in using prior knowledge. You'd be surprised at the amount of metaphor that is embedded in what we ask students to read. By definition, metaphorical understandings depend on prior knowledge. In science, we have all kinds of metaphors for linking that which is too vast, too small, too old, too fast, or too slow for our understanding to something that we do understand. In social studies, we have all kinds of metaphorical expressions: *pocket veto, mushroom cloud, McCarthyism, Watergate, a chicken in every pot, Open Door Policy,* and the *Underground Railroad,* to name just a few. The spatial models of math are metaphorical. And literature, it goes without saying, depends deeply on the readers' abilities to fuse their world with that of the story or poem by metaphorical understandings.

Summary: The Before Strategies

These are our three before-reading strategies:

- ◆ Establish a purpose for reading
- ◆ Preview, using textual features
- ◆ Bring forth prior knowledge, as related to the purpose for reading

6

The *During* Strategies

About the During-Reading Strategies

The next three strategies operate during reading to help the reader extract meaning from text. If the strategies work, they will hook up with the before-reading strategies to help the reader extract meaning from text.

1. The strategies keep the reader engaged and focused on the purpose for reading.

2. They use the reader's prior knowledge to continue to make meaningful connections.

3. They allow the reader to be aware when concentration and comprehension break down and have the ability to do what is necessary to repair gaps in comprehension.

During reading, readers need to engage in self-talk, which is called meta-reading. Meta-reading is thinking about reading while reading, just as metacognition is thinking about cognitive processes while engaging in those very processes (in other words, thinking about learning). The self-talk that we engage in while reading allows us to pick up the stitches of reading and know what to do when we drop the stitches. The following are some examples of meta-reader self-talk:

Syntax: Wait a minute. I'm losing this sentence. Let me go back and read it again, this time more slowly. Wait a minute. I still don't get it. Let me go back to the sentence before it and see if it makes sense. Wait a minute. What's the subject of this sentence, and what's the verb? Okay, now, I get it. I can move on.

Vocabulary: Oh, here's that word again. I still don't know what it means. Maybe I can figure it out by reading the surrounding sentences. Okay, here it is again. This time, I have more information about it. I guess it means_____. If I come across it again and it doesn't mean what I think it means, I can look it up.

Engagement, Focus, Concentration: Whoa, I blanked out here. I'm not picturing anything. What's going on? I'll have to go back and see where my mind started to wander.

If comprehension continues to elude the reader, then it's time for further action. Is the problem internal or external? Internal problems would be, for example, that the reader doesn't have sufficient prior knowledge to understand the text. If that is the case, then he or she would have to scaffold, go to another source such as the Internet, a previous chapter, a reading guide, or another person to fill in the gaps before continuing to read. If the reader does not bother to do this, then chances are, comprehension will not improve.

Is the internal problem psychological? Reading requires concentration and energy. Maybe now is just not the right time. Before setting aside the reading, however, (and running the risk of never returning to it), it's a great opportunity to at least establish that base coat of knowledge. The reader says, "Okay, I can't concentrate on this whole chapter now. I'll just read the headings and the first and last sentences of the major sections. That way, when I come back to it, at least I'll have something to hook new information to."

I want to stress the wisdom of this action. This reader has negotiated with the task. In giving it the mental energy that he or she has available, although limited, an investment in his or her knowledge bank has been made that will pay off when he or she returns to the task in a more receptive state of mind. And, something has been done now to make it easier to absorb the information later on.

Is the problem external? That is, do we have sensory interference, such as insufficient light, ambient noise, uncomfortable physical conditions? Reading is not a good competitor against other forces that would hijack the mind. Wise readers know what they need to be able to concentrate, and they either arrange their environment accordingly or else defer the reading task for a more availing time. The important thing is that wise readers do not fool themselves into believing that they have read when all they've done is adopt the posture of reading while thinking about something else while their eyes were on the page.

What do you do when you don't fully understand what you are reading? I reread, adjust my environment, try again to get an overview, read more slowly, get a pen and start circling things. If comprehension breakdown is really bad, I may have to fetch up more knowledge about what I'm reading: reference books, dictionaries, Web sites, colleagues. I may have to make an outline or other kind of organizer. The point is that I knew I wasn't understanding, and I think there's something that I can do about it. Deficient readers don't necessarily have awareness of either one of these conditions when comprehension breaks down for them.

We are about to examine the following three during-reading strategies:

1. Recognizing textual pattern clusters

2. Visualizing and animating

3. Making connections

These three strategies will allow the reader to self-monitor for comprehension and make adjustments to pace, environment, and mental preparedness.

During-Reading Strategy: Recognize Textual Pattern Clusters

Of all the strategies, this one takes the most time to explain, as we have eight major textual patterns to expose. They are as follows:

1. Narrative
2. Description
3. Classification
4. Definition
5. Exemplification
6. Cause and Effect
7. Comparison/Contrast
8. Process Analysis (sequence)

To make it easier to recognize the patterns, we can group them in accordance with how they usually go together:

♦ Narrative and description

♦ Classification, definition, exemplification

♦ Cause and effect, comparison/contrast

♦ Process analysis (sequence)

Before we go into how to recognize each of the pattern clusters, let me explain the importance of this strategy to get the reader back on track.

The brain likes to receive information that is organized. When we receive information that we think is not organized, we spend time trying to organize it so that we can find a place for it in our brain closet (schema). Using the metaphor of driving, think about how you drive on different kinds of roads: the interstate highway, two-lane county roads, winding country roads, suburban streets, main streets, and city streets. Knowing what kind of road you are on compresses all kinds of decisions about how you are to drive. What is likely to happen that you need to be read to defend against? How fast can you go? How familiar are the signs around you? Can you go on cruise control?

Now apply that to a reading situation in which you know what kind of textual pattern you are in. Once you know that, you can do the following:

- Establish a background and foreground. The background is going to be structural: wording that establishes the pattern. The foreground is going to be the specific information that increases your knowledge.

- Read faster because you can establish expectations. Every sentence is not a surprise.

- Read efficiently because you know where important information is to be found and the relationships that the information will have to the overall pattern.

- Read purposefully because you can determine whether or not the pattern is related to your purpose.

As a rule, a stretch of text will have a dominant pattern and a supportive one. For example, any kind of story will have a narrative pattern that is supported with description. A newspaper editorial will likely have a cause and effect pattern that is supported with comparison/contrast (or, the reverse, where the dominant pattern of the newspaper editorial is comparison/contrast, supported with cause and effect). A chapter in the biology textbook is likely to have a classification pattern, supported by definition and also by exemplification. A mathematics text and a foreign language text are likely to have process analysis (sequence) supported by definition and exemplification. The longer the text is, the more patterns we are likely to find within it.

Pattern-finding in text is often gray area work. It is the thinking process of trying to recognize the pattern that focuses us on the reading and unlocks meaning. It is not so important that every reader agree on what the dominant and supportive pattern is in gray area text. More important is that readers think about what the patterns might be, and in so doing, make meaning from text. So, don't spend inordinate time puzzling over whether cause and effect is the dominant or supportive pattern, or whether we are dealing more with description or classification. Understand that the fact that we are thinking about these things means we are already doing some important work in the text. Thus, pattern-finding in text is itself a vehicle for comprehension. That is why it is a strategy.

Pattern Cluster 1: Narrative and Description

The narrative pattern tells a story. A story is a self-contained journey (geographical or psychological) of a main character, who lives in a specified time and place, and who has a desire that is thwarted by one or more obstacles. The story ends on a resolution where the character's desire is either fulfilled or not fulfilled. Either way, the character is changed as a result of the journey, and his or her relationship to the motivating desire may have changed.

Narrative can be the overarching structure of a long piece of text, as it would be in a novel or biography. Or, it we can have mini-narratives that serve another dominant structure. We call those mini-narratives *anecdotes*, and they are similar to examples. A reader can certainly be given leeway if he or she names an anecdote as either supportive narrative or supportive example. Case studies are both narrative and example.

Of course, literature is where we find the most text having narrative structure. We also find narrative structure in social studies reading, although the main character may be a tribe or nation rather than an individual. Narratives are driven by the reader's connection to the main character and the reader's understanding of the motivational desire.

Following are two graphic organizers (see Figures 6.1 and 6.2) that help us recognize and understand narrative text:

Figure 6.1. Reading Comprehension Graphic Organizer 1

Somebody	*in*	*wanted*	*, but*	*so…*
Main Character	*Setting*	*Motivation*	*Obstacles/ Conflicts*	*Key Plot Events*

Figure 6.2. Reading Comprehension Graphic Organizer 2

Narrative

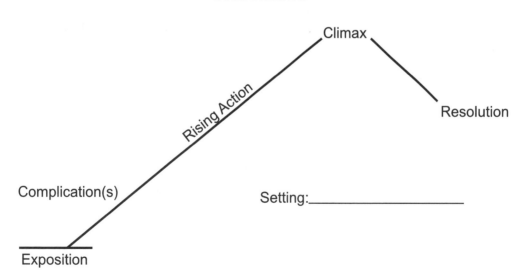

The descriptive pattern offers sensory and spatial detail. Because it is easy to overuse this pattern, to think that almost every text qualifies as "description," I suggest limiting the label *descriptive pattern* to only that which is either multisensory or that which offers undeniable, specific, and vivid visual images.

Any sustained narrative will be supported by description at several points. It is at the descriptive points that the reader is supposed to stop and look around, imaginatively, the way a camera pans a scene. Description can have a preponderance of state of being verbs to allow the scene to stay in place as the writer describes it. It can also use sense verbs such as *seem, appear, become, sound, look, smell, taste,* and *feel.* Of course, descriptive text can use action verbs as well, but only in service of description, not to advance the text. Writers very often use participles, adjectives that are derived from verbs and are serving adjectival purposes, in descriptive text. Look at the following example from Hal Borland's book of descriptive text about the seasons, *Sundial of the Seasons.* In this passage, Borland describes the beauty of October. I want you to notice how the description hangs on *to be* verbs, to pin October in place, but that the writer uses participial verb forms as adjectives that enliven the description without turning it into narrative:

 ## Example: Literary Description

> October is the year at rich maturity, a happy woman arrayed in festival dress and ready for a dance with a giant come down from the hills attired in a red, red shirt, buckskin pants and moccasins beaded with frost. October is a brisk wind in the treetops, a whisper among crisp leaves, a breath of apple cider, a gleam from a jack-'o-lantern, and the echo of laughter under a full moon
>
> October is bright as a bittersweet berry. October has the high excitement of a hunting dog's voice on the trail, the day-tang of walnut hulls and sumac berries, the night call of the owl and the bark of a restless fox. (Borland, p. 192)

Borland's description is heavily visual, but it also lets you experience the feel of October (i.e., *brisk wind*) and its sounds (i.e., *whisper among crisp leaves*) as well as its taste (i.e., *cider*).

Impatient readers can resent description. Their impatience with a key feature of fine literature is where several strategies converge: pattern recognition, visualization, and calling forth prior knowledge. Impatient readers need to understand that the purpose of description is to create the story world, not to advance the story, as narration does. However, when they recognize that the story has taken a pause for description, perhaps they can understand why the author has stopped to get them to look around.

Before we can characterize any text as *descriptive,* we have to justify that claim by showing multisensory references or the presence of so many visuals that the text can be justified as being descriptive in its major purpose The following graphic organizer (Figure 6.3) can move students away from just declaring that every kind of text is descriptive.

Figure 6.3. Description Organizer

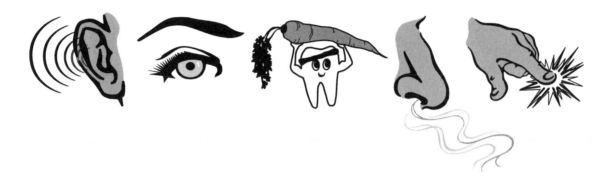

Pattern Cluster 2: Classification, Definition, Exemplification

English teachers spend a good portion of their time on narrative and description and so do elementary school teachers. But other, more fact-based text gets short shrift. Many of the specific skills necessary to make meaning from narrative and descriptive text are not transferable to those needed for straightforward information processing.

In science reading especially, we find a lot of classification, definition, and exemplification. These three forms go well together. Much of science is the learning about a taxonomy, and to learn a taxonomy, we learn about categories and their characteristics. That is classification. The words *kinds of* are the key clue that we are reading classification. Others clue words are *attributes, features, characteristics, type, sort, example.* What you are reading right now is classification, as I have classified the various text patterns into clusters and am explaining the features of each cluster. Sorting is a critical thinking skill. When we establish a taxonomy and sort items into categories, we are evaluating against criteria, and that is a high level thinking skill (see Figure 6.4).

Figure 6.4. Features Matrix

	Classification				

The graphic organizer for classification may be familiar to students as a *features matrix*, as it is called in math and science classes. A features matrix for the planets would display the names of the planets (Mercury, Venus, Earth, Mars, Jupiter, etc.) on the first horizontal line and features (e.g., size, speed of rotation, closeness to sun, etc.), vertically.

A definition has three parts: the first isolates the target word or phrase; the second places that word or phrase into a domain; the third establishes how the target word or phrase can be distinguished from other members of its domain. We can classify definitions, as well. First, we have a dictionary definition. That kind of definition is usually not included in text. We find it in isolation in a dictionary or glossary. What we are more likely to encounter in text are working definitions and extended definitions. A working definition is a definition that will serve a situational purpose. It takes the dictionary definition and makes it more pliable to suit the manner in which we decide to put a word to work in discourse. Working definitions are set forth at the outset of discourse so that writer and audience can agree on how a particular word or term is going to be used.

An extended definition can go on for a paragraph or even for an entire essay if the writer's purpose is to craft a very complex idea. Ideas such as "national security," "the ideal form of public education," and "the most important environmental issue of the 21st century" are examples of topics that could be developed through extended definition.

The following graphic organizer (Figure 6.5) can be used to recognize and analyze a definition.

Figure 6.5. Definition Organizer

Definition

_____ is
(subject, expressed as a noun)

_____ that
(Place the subject into a general category.)

Name the specific characteristics of the subject that distinguish it from other
  members of its category.

_____

_____

_____

Exemplification

It stands to reason that when you encounter a definition you can soon encounter one or more examples. Examples concretize the definition and therefore most readers find them a welcome addition. Writers often explicitly point out examples through the use of *for example, for instance, such as,* or the Latin abbreviation *e.g.* Examples, as I mentioned earlier, can also be anecdotes (mini-narratives).

The following graphic organizer (Figure 6.6) can be used to recognize and process examples, and to generate more examples than the text provides.

Figure 6.6. Example Organizer

Example

_____ is an example of

_____.

(its features) _____

_____

_____

The pattern cluster of classification, definition, and example is extremely common in content area text, albeit far less common in the kinds of texts read in English class. If you teach a class that has a lot of classification, definition, and example, don't let students fall into the habit of saying that classification is description. To do so (and it's tempting to do so) allows the missed opportunity of learning the definitions and clarifying them with examples.

Example: Literary Description

Again, see Hal Borland, this time writing in the classification mode:

> The birds gather for migration, restless and gregarious, busy but nowhere near so full of song as they were three months ago. In a pasture beside a woodland are at least two dozen flickers, which we do not often think of as flock birds. Down the road is a congregation of robins. High overhead, riding the thermals above the ridges, are half a dozen hawks putting on an aerial display that makes one catch his breath in wonder, Restless, all of them with the inner urge that will soon send them southward."

Any time we have an array of something, in this case migratory birds, and the author is delineating members or parts, let's call that classification.

Cluster Pattern 3:
Cause and Effect and Comparison/Contrast

In a way, cause and effect is a kind of comparison/contrast because you're comparing something as it was before the cause brought about the effect. These two forms are very substantial forces in all content-area writing, so recognizing them is a key reading skill.

In addition to being embedded in academic texts, cause and effect questions are the backbone of multiple choice, short constructed response, and essay questions. Think about how many questions prompt a cause and effect answer:
Why…

Give two causes of…

Give three reasons for…

Explain the effects of….

Discuss one positive and one negative effect of…

We can think of cause and effect as the "what and why." The "what and why" are embedded in narrative as well as informational text. The words *so, because, cause, therefore, thus, hence, explain(s),result,* and *why* are cues to the presence of cause and effect. A more sophisticated cause and effect pattern is the syllogism, that is, the *if/then* statement. The straightforward syllogism is foundational in mathematics text. We can also think of cause and effect as "reason and result."

The following very simple graphic organizer (Figure 6.7) can be used to help readers recognize cause and effect text.

Figure 6.7. Cause and Effect Organizer

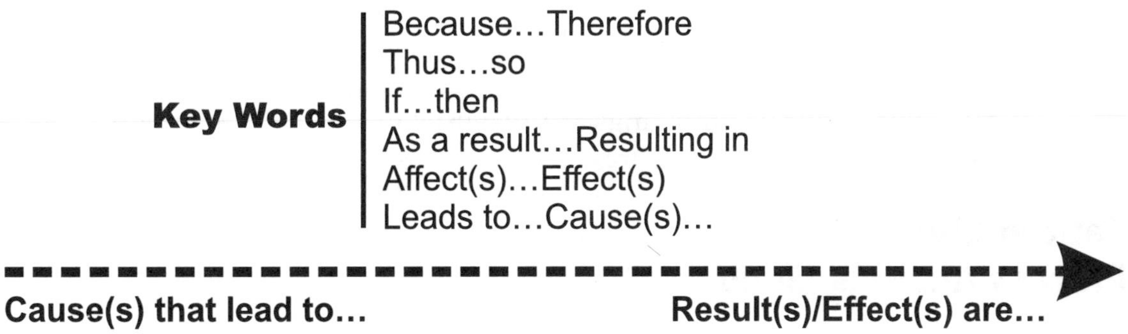

Key Words
- Because…Therefore
- Thus…so
- If…then
- As a result…Resulting in
- Affect(s)…Effect(s)
- Leads to…Cause(s)…

Cause(s) that lead to…   **Result(s)/Effect(s) are…**

Comparison/Contrast is an essential text pattern because we understand new information through what we already know. Therefore, when new information comes along, the mental process that finds a place in the brain closet (schema) for that new information is a process involving comparison/contrast.

Key words signaling the contrast structure are *but, however, on the one hand, on the other hand, in contrast, although, even though, different.* Key words signaling similarities are *and, also, additionally, in addition, similar to, another, same.* Students should be taught to keep their eyes peeled for these words and set up a mental visual cue to help them arrange the items and attributes that are being compared and contrasted.

The following very simple graphic organizer (Figure 6.8) can be used to help readers recognize comparison/contrast text.

Figure 6.8. Comparison/Contrast Organizer

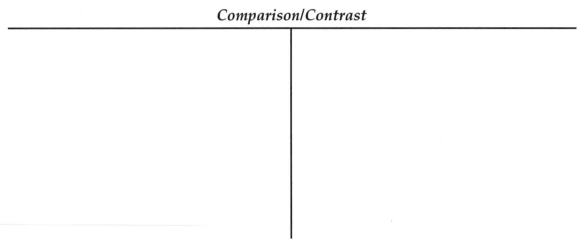

Comparison/Contrast

Venn diagrams of two or three rings are also used extensively as a math application for processing comparison/contrast relationships.

Pattern Cluster 4: Process Analysis (Sequence)

The last of the pattern clusters is process analysis, or sequence. This pattern is found most explicitly in mathematics text, where the steps of a procedure are laid out one by one. We also find process analysis text in foreign language textbooks on pages where the student is being shown how to create word morphologies, such as noun declensions or verb conjugations. Process analysis is like a recipe in which each step begins with a verb. Usually, process analysis text is easy to recognize because the steps are laid out in list form.

The following simple graphic organizer (Figure 6.9) can be used to help students recognize process analysis text.

Figure 6.9. Process Analysis Organizer

Ideally, all students would be provided with visuals, such as the preceding graphic organizers, for the pattern clusters. Each of the clusters should be color-coded:

Narrative and description: **yellow**

Classification, definition, exemplification: **pink**

Cause and effect, comparison/contrast: **blue**

Process analysis: **green**

If such visuals were school-wide, with the same posters in every classroom as a ready reference, the cue to readers would be very strong, as would the unified message that *the teachers in this school are here to help you access learning by building reading strategies.* For your school to post universal visuals would be inexpensive and unobtrusive and would provide a powerful reminder of a simple strategy for students to use to find their way during reading.

Example: Social Studies Text

Lord-Peasant Relationships in England Before and After the Black Death

Most land was owned by the nobility (the lords) or by the church. Peasants did not have the freedom to move to another location. If land was sold or transferred from one lord to another, the peasants were part of the purchase.

Each peasant family had the use of 30 acres of land for growing their own food and limited use of pastureland for raising a few animals. The same 30 acres were handed down to the peasant's sons, generation after generation. The fields were planted, cultivated, and harvested according to the plans set by the lord.

Peasants were usually required to work three days per week on the lord's farmland. During the harvesting of the lord's fields, additional work was required of all members of the peasant's family. The lord's officials supervised the work, trying to make sure that peasants worked as hard as possible. In addition to work, the peasant owed the lord various payments at specific times during the year, such as a goose or chicken at Christmas. His daughters could not marry without payment to the lord. And when the peasant died, his family was required to give his best animal to the lord.

Changes Following the Black Death

The great decrease in the number of peasants available to work the land caused by the Black Death led to drastic changes in the relationship between lord and peasant. Conflicts between peasants wanting a better deal and lords trying to keep the old relationship intact led in England to the Peasants' Revolt of 1381. The leaders of the revolt demanded that the customary obligations of peasants be abolished in exchange for a fixed rent payment. Although the Peasants' Revolt did not succeed in 1381, over the next few decades the lords were forced to grant more freedoms to the peasants.

By the early 1400s, independent farmers producing for the market, and paying fixed money rents to the lords for the use of their land, had replaced peasants tied to the land. These farmers were free to farm their land as they chose, rather than having to follow the lord's methods. They and their children were also free to move to another lord's territory, or to move to the growing towns and cities and seek work there.

Social Studies

Why a Student Might Have Difficulty Comprehending This Text

The reader has to see that the purpose of this text is to contrast in two ways: the lord and peasant relationship is contrasted, and the feudal relationship between these two groups before and after the Black Death is contrasted. The failure to perceive these two points of contrast would be a failure in comprehension. Of course, implicit in the comparison/contrast is a cause and effect relationship, with the cause being the Black Death, and the effect being the decimation of the peasant population, and the effect of *that* being the Peasant's Revolt. In turn, the effect of *that event* would be emergence of independent farmers, and the effect of *that* would be the social mobility that resulted in the growth of towns and cities.

Mini-Lesson: Mrs. Jackson on Reading Comparison/Contrast and Cause and Effect

"I'm going to ask you to read this page about how the Black Death changed the relationship between the lords and the

> Understand comparison/contrast text

peasants in the fourteenth century. As you read this, think about the contrasts. The contrast between the lords and the peasants should always be clear in your mind as you read. If you're not thinking about that contrast, stop reading and go back to where you stopped thinking about it. You'll find that, as you read, there is still contrast between the lords and the peasants, but after the Black Death, the contrast turns into conflict and the conflict brings about change. So, as you're reading, think about how this page is about contrast, conflict, change."

Analysis

Mrs. Jackson has asked students to keep in mind a central theme of social studies: contrast, conflict, change. (Sometimes, there is no change after the conflict, as when things go back to the way they were before the conflict.) Mrs. Jackson is instilling in the students an essential habit of mind that will help them focus on the main idea not only for this text, but throughout the year and in future years.

Example: Science Text

Steps of the Scientific Method

1. *Statement of the problem:* The problem is stated as a question.

2. *Proposal of a Hypothesis:* A hypothesis is a prediction, also called an educated guess, about the answer to the problem. The hypothesis serves as a guide for what kind of data is to be collected and how it should be interpreted. The scientist is not supposed to have a vested interest in whether or not the hypothesis turns out to be true. If he or she does have such a vested interested, then he or she could be said to be biased. Scientific conclusions must be unbiased.

3. *Test of the Hypothesis.* A controlled experiment is designed to test the hypothesis. In a controlled experiment, only one factor will be tested. This one factor to be tested is called the variable. A parallel experiment, without the variable, must be conducted. The factors, procedures, and conditions in the parallel experiment are called the control group, or just the control. It is absolutely essential that the two experiments are the same in every way except for the variable that is being tested.

4. *Observations:* The scientist now observes and records. The records are called data. Data must be meticulously recorded. Data may take various forms, such as measurements, countable quantities, quantifiable changes. The data must be organized and represented by a diagram, table, chart, graph, or other visual pattern that is understandable by another scientist. The data, once presented, may lead to a conclusion (answer to the question) or to a further hypothesis. The scientist must be completely open to and accepting of the fact that the date may not support the hypothesis and may yield a surprising conclusion.

5. *Statement of conclusion:* A conclusion is valid only if it is supported by sufficient data, is objective (separating fact from opinion), is drawn from adequate evidence, is unbiased, and follows logically from the given evidence. The statement of conclusion is the answer to the original question.

6. *Replication:* Scientists offer the information about their experiments to the scientific community (other scientists) so that other scientists can test the conclusions. The repetition of the exact same procedures using the exact same variables under the exact same conditions is called replication. If the results of an experiment remain constant after numerous replications, then the results of the experiment become scientific law. Even then, however, scientists remain open to new information that may alter their beliefs about what is and is not scientific law.

Why a Student Might Have Difficulty Comprehending This Text

The difficulty in constructing the intended meaning from text such as this lies in the reader's ability to form extremely narrow (domain-specific) definitions of the key terms: *scientific method, method, variable, test, conclusion, control*. Words such as these have vernacular meanings that must be kept separate from their domain-specific meanings.

This information is, of course, at the heart of scientific study. The steps of the scientific method are, in effect, the Constitution of science, the backbone document against which all knowledge will judged true or not true. The scientific method, as delineated here, will serve as an evaluative touchstone: Any experiment or conclusion or scientific law will be measured against its tenets.

Yet, the scientific method, as text, does not come alive until the reader is either engaged in its steps or evaluating a conclusion. For that reason, it can be difficult to comprehend without an example of a problem, hypothesis, procedure, data, recording, and conclusion to animate it.

Mini-Lesson: Mr. Howard on Process Analysis Text

"A lot of what we read in science tells you the steps of how to do something, like a recipe. Sometimes, you're reading and doing at the

> Understanding reading about a process by visualizing the steps

same time, going back and forth. But other times, you can be reading about a process that you are not doing at that time. That is what we have here, with this explanation of the scientific method. So, because you have to read about the steps of doing something that you are not doing as you're reading, I want you to *imagine* that you are following the steps. That will help you focus on the meaning. And, so that you can focus on what you are imagining, I want you to take notes as you read. Set up a table: two columns, six rows. In the left-hand column, write the key words of the six steps of the scientific method. In the right-hand column, you're going to write what you would be doing in an actual scientific investigation."

Analysis

Mr. Howard is requiring the students to process meaning as they read, to translate theoretical information into actions. What he is having the students do with the text is much more effective than having them "read and take a quiz."

Understanding Through Pattern Clusters

Use these guiding questions to get students inside the texts that they are reading. Once students have, with your help, identified the main and supportive organizing schemes (i.e., pattern clusters), they can unlock meaning by answering these questions. The questions should cue them to think deeply about how recognizing the organizing scheme allows the reader to extract meaning.

Remember our pattern clusters:

- Narrative and description
- Classification, definition, exemplification
- Cause and effect
- Comparison/Contrast
- Process analysis (sequence)

Decide which of these pattern clusters is the *main* organizational structure of the piece. Then, decide which of these pattern clusters is a *supportive* structure of the piece.

Note: There may be more than one correct answer possible.

1. *Narrative and description:* How is the piece developed through narrative? That is, how does a story develop from beginning to end? Who are the characters in the story? What is their relationship to each other? What is the setting of the story? In the descriptive parts of the story, what is being described? What are the key words used to describe it? What senses does the writer refer to in the description? What parts of the description are particularly memorable?

2. *Classification, definition, exemplification:* What things are being classified? What are the categories in the classification? What common traits do the members of each category share? What key terms are defined? What examples are given?

3. *Cause and effect:* Connect cause(s) to effect(s). In other words, what causes what? Does the text tell you why? Cause and effect text is closely related to comparison/contrast because cause and effect is about changing. What can you say about the difference between the subject before and after its change?

4. *Comparison/Contrast:* What things are being compared and contrasted? What are the similarities between them? What are the differences? Often, comparison/contrast text involves cause and effect. Do you see a cause and effect relationship in the text?

5. *Process analysis (sequence):* Why are each of the steps necessary?

During-Reading Strategy: Making Connections

If learning equals the integration of new information with existing knowledge, then learning happens when we make connections.

In *Mosaic of Thought*, Zimmermann and Keene talk about three kinds of connections that readers should be encouraged to make as they read:

1. *Text-to-Text:* These are connections between what we are reading and what we've read before, either elsewhere in the book that we are reading, or elsewhere in the reading world.

2. *Text-to-Self:* These are connections between what we are reading and our own experience, knowledge, and emotions.

3. *Text-to-World:* These are connections between what we are reading and current events of the community, nation, and world as well as connections to history.

The connection-making process keeps us engaged in what we are reading and keeps us mindful that reading is a meaning-making process. Figure 6.10 offers some questions that readers can ask themselves to make these three kinds of connections.

Figure 6.10. Making Connections

Text-to-Text Questions	
Where have I read something like this before?	
What are the unfamiliar words and phrases?	
What parts of these words and phrases have I seen before?	
Have I seen words and phrases like this in a different class?	
Text-to-Self Questions	
What would I think if what is told about in this text happened to me?	
What would I feel if what is told about in this text happened to me?	
Did I ever experience anything like this?	
Did anyone that I know personally ever experience anything like this?	

Text-to-World Questions	
Does this remind me of anything going on in my school?	
Does this remind me of anything going on in my community?	
Does this remind me of anything that I hear about in the news?	
Does this remind me of anything that I've learned about in history?	

Remember that the strategies can't just be used perfunctorily. They have to be used for their intended purpose of extracting meaning from text, and not just any meaning, the author's intended meaning. Don't fall into the thoughtless habit of letting students make irrelevant connections between text, self, and world without developing the conscious understanding of how those connections are helping them achieve *useful* understanding.

 Example: Social Studies Text

How Railroads Changed America

It would be hard to overestimate the significance of the railroads on America's economy in the years after the Civil War. The iron, steel, and coal industries boomed in the 1870s and 1880s, supplying materials for the 150,000 miles of railroad tracks that would link American cities. With transportation comes communication, and the railroad industry was a boon to the telegraph industry, with telegraph lines springing up along the tracks. The railroads changed the way food was brought to the American table, with the cattle and meat-packing industries, as well as the farmers, delivering food by rail to food markets nationwide.

Because railroads made it possible to deliver goods to places formerly inaccessible, the entire economy changed. Whereas before railroads, towns and cities had to be largely economically independent, small monopolies thrived. But with the delivery of goods from distant places, competition became the order of the day. Goods could be purchased from the burgeoning numbers of traveling salesmen. They offered what was then a vast array of merchandise from catalogs such as Sears, Roebuck, and Montgomery Ward.

Social Studies

When forces are introduced into a society that change transportation and communication, other changes happen as well. The railroads made it possible for people from all geographical parts of the country to see other parts of America's geography and subcultures as never before. Chicago, the major railroad hub of the country, boomed as a great American city based on trade. The train schedule eclipsed the sun as a way of telling time, and the wristwatch became a staple in Americans' list of possessions (to be bought at Sears, of course). Traveling circuses and other diversions, including political campaigns, brought a national cultural awareness to small towns.

Why a Student Might Have Difficulty Comprehending This Text

This text is about a cause and effect relationship, not just a series of examples. The reader has to apply the principle, stated directly as the first sentence of the third paragraph, that forces that change transportation and communication bring unprecedented growth in the ways that people live. This is a major social studies concept, and the reader needs to see it as a recurrent theme that applies to today's world, the post Civil War era, and ancient history.

Mini-Lesson: Mr. Lee on Making Connections during Reading

"This week, we're going to be reading about how the railroads changed America in the post Civil War years. You'll be reading about many examples, but I want you to think about how cell phones are like railroads."

Helping students make connections to their own lives.

The students smile.

Mr. Lee goes on to say, "No, cell phones don't run on tracks and, no, railroads don't allow you to text message your friends, but both cell phones and railroads changed the way people are able to communicate with each other, and both cell phones and railroads changed the way people thought about physical distance.

"Make a list of all the ways your life would change if all of a sudden, you didn't have a cell phone, and no one else did either."

He gives the students a few minutes to make their lists in their notebooks. "Okay, because you understand what your life would be like without cell phones, you understand how cell phones changed the way we live. If you understand that, then you can understand how railroads changed the way people lived in the 19th century. So, you understand the ideas in the chapter, you just don't know the details. Now, when you are reading this chapter in the textbook, I want you to stop and think about your list, and think about how you already showed that you understand what this chapter is all about."

Analysis

Mr. Lee has done a great job of hooking the students into the social studies text about the rise of the railroads by connecting (pardon the pun) them to a feature that has changed modern life. Of course, most of his students can't even imagine what life was like before cell phones, and that is why his lesson is so meaningful: It teaches the theme of social change resulting from technology by using both a historical and a contemporary example. It is also a great example of creative thinking, which can be defined as making new combinations brought together with a common theme.

 ## Example: English Language Arts Text

> **Excerpted from "The Open Window" by Saki**
>
> "My aunt will be down presently, Mr. Nuttel," said a very self-possessed young lady of fifteen: "in the meantime you must try and put up with me."
>
> Framton Nuttel endeavored to say the correct something that should duly flatter the niece of the moment without unduly discounting the aunt that was to come. Privately he doubted more than ever whether these formal visits on a succession of total strangers would do much towards helping the nerve cure which he was supposed to be undergoing.
>
> "I know how it will be, " his sister had said when he was preparing to migrate to this rural retreat: "you will bury yourself down there and not speak to a living soul, and your nerves will be worse than ever from moping. I shall just give you letters of introduction to all the people I know there. Some of them, as far as I can remember, were quite nice."
>
> Framton wondered whether Mrs. Sappleton, the lady to whom he was presenting one of the letters of introduction, came into the nice division.

Why a Student Might Have Difficulty Comprehending This Text

The exposition of a work of fiction is always difficult for students who have trouble with reading comprehension because there's no story yet to hang onto. It's like going into a new place without any orientation. You don't have your bearings, you look around, and you don't see anyone you know; you don't want to make a fool of yourself by your ignorance, and you just want to leave in a hurry. That is how the reluctant reader feels at the start of a story.

Mini-Lesson:
Ms. Roper on Making Connections

"The beginning of a story is always the hardest part to get into. You're meeting new people in new places, and you don't know why you're there. The trick is to make a connection right away. Find something familiar. Go with the 1 percent rule. The 1 percent rule states that after you've read only 1 percent of a story, whether that be a short story, such as this one, or a longer piece such as a novel, you should stop and make three kinds of connections after you've read 1 percent. This story in the textbook takes up about four pages, so your 1 percent comes in after the first few sentences. In a 350-page novel, your 1 percent would be after the first 3 pages. These are your three connections:

Connections between the students' own lives and the themes in a work of fiction

"Connection one: What have I read that reminds me of this? Connection two: What has happened to me that reminds me of this? Connection three: What has happened in the world, today or in history, that reminds me of this?

"If you can't make all three connections, make at least *one.*"

Analysis

Mrs. Roper has found a way to encourage students to continue with their reading when they get discouraged, and she knows that discouragement often comes *very early* in the reading experience, hence her 1 percent rule. In the case of this story, she expects that the students will have some difficulty getting into the story because of its British-sounding language and leisurely pace. However, she knows that they are capable of relating the story to a time when they were uncomfortable meeting a stranger in unfamiliar surroundings or a time when they felt anxious about a meeting. By offering three connections and then reducing the choices to at least one, Mrs. Roper allows the students to feel that they have some choice, something accessible to them. Had she suggested just one connection, many of the students would have been resistant even to that, but by whittling the challenge down from three, which may seem overwhelming, to one, which seems compromising, we stand a better chance with the students.

The following are some tips for teaching the during-reading strategy of making connections:

♦ Suggest that students develop the habit of saying, "This reminds me of _____ " as they read and especially when they lose focus.

- Encourage students to pick up dropped stitches in their comprehension by saying to themselves, "Because I understand _____, I can understand _____."

- Encourage the use of double-sided journals. On the left side, students write what they think are key points or interesting points; on the right side, they write personal connections, questions, opinions. (These are also called *reader response* journals)

- Read aloud to students and model what goes on inside your head as you make the three kinds of connections.

- Make students aware of the pitfall that sometimes the connections that they make while reading are the very things that distract them, so they have to be careful to stay focused.

- For literary text, make students aware that they are supposed to be forming emotional attachments—likes or dislikes—for the characters and settings. They should be asking themselves if they like and agree with characters or if they don't.

- For social studies text, make students aware that they should be always connecting the struggles that they are reading about to struggles and challenges in their world and community.

- Encourage students to do comparison/contrast thinking as they read. A form of connection can be made by noting a contrast as well as a similarity.

- The text-to-self connections are easiest to make, and they can be the most meaningful. But they are also the most limiting in terms of the students' development. Encourage those text-text and text-world connections.

- Debrief as a class by having students share their connections at a point during reading, if you are doing the reading in class. Make "connection paddles" out of sticky notes on ice cream sticks and have students hold them up at a designated connection-sharing time.

During-Reading Strategy: Visualizing and Animating

Visualizing and mentally animating text is a way of staying engaged, making the abstract concrete, making the reading experience memorable. Visualizing and animating text is a habit of mind. Habits are not developed because they are taught once. Habits develop over time, with consistent reminders.

It can be said that if you're not visualizing and animating then you're not reading. I can't imagine reading without doing the meaning-making mental activity of visualizing. But, that's because I'm a lifelong reader, and, although I consider myself a slow reader, not always a very attentive one, I developed the habit long ago of making characters and settings come alive in my head. My habit of visualizing and animating is my strongest link to the text. It's what brings me back when my comprehension fails me.

We say that the strategy is visualizing and animating, but actually it's a strategy of using as many senses as possible to animate the text. Sensory experiences are powerful learning triggers. Readers need to actively look for sensory cues. Most of these will be found in literary text. Literary text is the kind of text that lends itself most clearly to the strategy of visualization and animation, but other content area texts do as well, if less obviously. Ironically, or, maybe not so ironically, novels are usually without visuals (except, of course, for picture books). The visuals are expected to be supplied mentally, whereas, other content area books are richly supplied with all kinds of visuals.

The habit of visualizing enriches and elaborates on the text. You visualize what is there *plus* details of environment that may not be there. Everyone has had the experience of saying "The book was much better than the movie." For one thing, a movie is almost always shorter and less complex than a book. Also, a movie can't play the internal monologues, opening up the characters' heads the way a novel can. But, beyond this, we often resent movies about books we've enjoyed because movie-makers gives you what their imaginations supplied, and you like your imagination's version better. Imagination is part of the joy of reading about people, places, and adventures.

You need to reinforce the visualization strategy by modeling what goes on in your head as you read, having students translate text into drawings, having students exchange descriptions of what they visualized as they read or were read to. You can kill two birds with one stone if you stress the importance of using content-area vocabulary and words straight from the text to have these book to mind's eye to voice conversations.

Take visualization one step further by including emotion. Learning is strongly linked to emotion. Emotion triggers memory. Learning comes alive when it has an emotional piece, whether that be empathy, excitement, thrill of suspense, or sense of humor. We know from brain research that the mind captures the cognitive information along with the sensory and emotional experiences that come along with it. We need to experience reading with more than cognition. We need to bring in the senses and emotions.

Example: Social Studies Text

The Growth of American Cities and Towns

As the nineteenth century began in America, a new kind of labor was developing that would profoundly change the way Americans lived. This new kind of labor was the factory system, and it established a presence not only in the city but also in the countryside. Machine-based industries cropped up in rural areas, particularly around waterfalls. Mills, furnaces, and forges were dependent on water power to drive the machinery. It was this kind of water power that operated American industrial machinery until the Civil War, when steam power replaced it.

Because of the close ties between agriculture and the mills, it was the farmers who, along with local carpenters, developed the water powered mills in rural areas. These rural mills then caused their locations to grow into villages and towns having a general store to service the houses that would be built near the mill. Then, you'd get the blacksmith, the church, post office, and other services. Massachusetts would see the development of the industrial city of Lowell.

Why a Student Might Have Difficulty Comprehending This Text

This text requires readers to imagine the landscape as being different from what it is now. It is a good example of how a mini-lesson on visualization and animation can enhance comprehension.

Mini-Lesson: Mr. Ortega's Before and After Visualization

"We're going to read the section in the textbook that is about the growth of industry and the factory system in the nineteenth

> Activating visualization: "The movie in the mind"

century. To understand what you're reading, you have to picture it. Picture farmlands near a waterfall: what descriptive words can you think of that describe that scene?"

Students call out a few phrases and the teacher writes them on the board: *greenery, rows of plantings, rolling hills, spray, some farm machinery, white water, crystal rivers.* Mr. Ortega establishes that, looking at this list, we would characterize the images as *serene* and *beautiful.*

"Okay, now let's imagine a mill being built near that waterfall, and a factory that makes textiles. Let's imagine the workers in that factory, and the owners, the bosses. How do the workers get to the factory? Where did they come from before they worked there? Where do they live? Let's make a list of what we're seeing now, and how we would characterize it."

The students can see that the natural serenity and beauty of the rural countryside is changed into something that is crowded, man-made, angular, closed-off, and dark.

"Now, when you read this section of the chapter, picture what industrialization looks like and acts like."

Analysis

Mr. Ortega's simple mini-lesson is effective because it uses visualization and animation to access comprehension of the most important idea in the upcoming reading: The dramatic differences between rural and industrial regions, and how one turns into the other because of geographical features, such as a waterfall.

Mr. Ortega did not have to be a reading teacher to activate the imagination of his students so that the reading would come alive for them. This little mini-lesson—to get students to visualize and animate the transition from a rural to an industrial space, is something that he was going to do anyway—but he thought he could do it *after* the assigned reading. The trouble was, the students didn't do the reading, or, if they did, they had no mental pictures or actions as they did so. Sometimes, it is only the *timing* of a lesson—placing it before, rather than after, the assigned reading, that transforms it into what we would call a reading mini-lesson. Mr. Ortega did not sacrifice any social studies instruction to give this mini-lesson, and yet it helped his students develop the strategy of visualizing and animating while reading.

 Example: English Language Arts Text

> **Antigone**
>
> Listen, Ismene:
> Creon buried our brother Eteocles
> With military honors, gave him a soldier's funeral.
> And it was right that he should; but Polyneices,
> Who fought as bravely and died as miserably,—
> They say that Creon has sworn
> No one shall bury him, no one mourn for him,
> But his body must lie in the fields, as sweet treasure
> For carrion birds to find as they search for food.
> That is what they say, and our good Creon is coming here

English Language Arts

> To announce it publicly; and the penalty—
> Stoning to death in the public square!
>   There it is,
> And now you can prove what you are:
> A true sister, or a traitor to your family.

Mini-Lesson:
Mrs. Dalton's Mind's Eye Theater

Mrs. Dalton has given the students a copy of this speech, so that they can mark the text. "Let's visualize what's happening. Use your

Activating visualization: "the movie in the mind"

highlighter to identify the noun phrases that give you specific pictures."

The students highlight the noun phrases, *with military honors, a soldier's funeral, his body …in the fields, carrion birds,* and so on.

"Okay, now use a different color highlighter to identify the actions that are named by the verb phrases. The students highlight lying *in the fields, search for food, stoning to death, fought, mourn.*

Mrs. Dalton continues: "Okay, that's good. We can picture what is going on in this very dramatic scene. What are the things that are happening as Antigone speaks, and what are the things that someone hearing her would have to imagine? Let's separate the time zones.

The students say that the only thing that is happening as Antigone speaks to Ismene is that Antigone is speaking to Ismene. Everything else would be happening in her, and in the audience's imagination.

"What Sophecles is doing," Mrs. Dalton explains, "is setting up a movie in the mind of the audience. He is using words to create horrible images of Eteocles's body being exposed to the elements, eaten by carrion birds. We're not actually seeing that, except in our mind's eye. Let's call that *mind's eye theater.* As you read *Antigone,* be aware of the difference between something that you would actually be seeing onstage, such as Antigone speaking to Ismene in this scene, and mind's eye theater: scenes that don't actually take place, but are described to get you to imagine them. The theater is already imagination. Mind's eye theater is imagination within imagination.

Analysis

Mrs. Dalton has taught the reading strategy of visualization and animation here by explaining a very common technique of fiction writers, and one that readers need to be aware of if they are to follow the frames within a narrative. Stories are almost always told in multiple time zones: The narrative moves forward with events, but the characters often take the reader back to past events, activating what Mrs. Dalton is calling "mind's eye theater." Some critical thinking questions are: Why did the playwright choose to convey this scene through mind's eye theater, rather than by just making it happen on the stage? If you were making a movie, would you show this image, or do you think it is more powerful to have the viewer imagine it?

As with the earlier social studies lesson, this lesson becomes a reading enhancement lesson when it *precedes* the reading, cueing the reader to visualize and to notice the existence of mind's eye theater. The lesson could just as easily be placed after the reading, but then it would lose its power to inform the reader's experience during reading.

 ## Example: Science Text

Wetlands are a value to society. Wetlands provide for floodwater storage, biodiversity, natural beauty, and a habitat for fish and other wildlife. The ecosystem of the wetland is essential to human habitation. When humans disrupt the ecosystem of the wetlands, we risk great damage to developed land.

A wetland is a kind of natural sponge, absorbing and storing water that would otherwise flood areas of human habitation. The wetland slowly releases this water, and enables humans to rely on the areas where they have built homes and other buildings. Because of the wetlands, floodwaters become less of a damaging force of erosion or sudden devastation. During dry periods, the storage of floodwaters by the wetlands allows for the release of groundwater to surface water systems. The U.S. Army Corps of Engineers has determined that because the wetlands along the Charles River in Boston were protected, 17 million dollars of property damage was averted because of flood control.

The wetland ecosystem creates a slow rate of flow of water having potential pollutants. This pollutant-laden water settles on the wetland floor, away from the danger that it would pose if such pollutants were to be absorbed by plant roots and microorganisms in the soil. In this way, the wetlands act as a water filtration system. In fact, the water filtration provided by wetlands is so efficient that artificial wetlands have been built to manage potential pollutants after storms.

Science

Why a Student Might Have Difficulty Comprehending This Text

This cause-and-effect text might be difficult for a student who has no mental picture of wetlands. Comprehension of the text depends largely on being able to visualize and animate the movement of water through an ecosystem and the understanding of filtration, a process that can easily be demonstrated through visuals.

Mini-Lesson: Mr. Bell Demonstrating the Visuals in the Text

Mr. Bell is an earth science teacher who believes that his subject is richly visual and sensory. He always tries to connect theoretical

> Activating visualization by evoking a physical sensation

understandings to concrete experiences of the outdoors. Before assigning this reading, Mr. Bell brings in two visuals: a sponge and a water filtration system. His mini-lesson is simply to cue the students to visualize these two devices as they read. He also shows them pictures of wetlands to help them visualize. He asks them to list as many things as they can think of that would be in a wetland. "As you are reading," he says, pretend that you are in the wetland. Feel what it would feel like, feel what it would feel like, smell what it would smell like. Then you'll be able to focus on what you're reading."

Analysis

This teacher has taken no time away from his subject, the ecological value of wetlands, to coax the reading habit of visualizing text as a strategy to focus during reading. It's clear that the mini-lessons that encourage the strategy of visualizing and animating during reading to stay focused *also* provide the background knowledge. Not only that, but the mini-lesson also introduces key vocabulary that the students will encounter in the upcoming reading segment.

Using Visualization and Animation When the Text Provides Illustrations

As I've said, science and math texts can be *worked at* more than *read* if they are to be used to solve immediate problems. In science texts, illustrations are often provided to clarify the words. Many of these visuals are models, such as models or atomic structure, and the models themselves are part of the universal language of the subject. In other words, if you are learning about physics, that model of atomic structure is going to be presented to the students throughout the course, and they are going to be expected to decode it, just as if it were words on a page. As with math, in science, the illustrations become the language of the subject. To understand the subject, the student has to develop skills in two kinds of reading: reading the words and reading the visual models. Proficient readers in these subjects soon learn to conjure mental pictures of the models as they read the words.

Mini-Lesson:
Mr. Eamon's Visualizing Math Word Problems

Oh, those word problems! "I know how to do the math," says the frustrated student. "I just can't figure out what math to do." The key

Activating visualization through manipulatives

to solving the word problem is extracting something that looks like math from something that looks like words. Conditional statements often lurk in plain sight in word problems.

Example: Reading Math Word Problems

1. If the set of integers is the replacement set, what is the greatest value of x that makes the sentence $7x - 6 < 8$ a true statement?

2. Alison needs $80 to buy a cell phone. Her aunt paid her $25 for baby-sitting. If she saves $10 a week, what is the least number of weeks she would have to save to have enough money to buy the cell phone?

3. The Parkers have lived in Pine Hills 5 years longer than the Stevensons. If the sum of their years in Pine Hills is not more than 37 years, what is the greatest number of years that the Stevenson's residence in Pine Hills can be?

Why a Student Might Have
Difficulty Comprehending This Text

A good math reader/student can do these problems by seeing the math sentences in them. A not-so-good math reader/student needs explicit instruction about key words that are clues to what kind of math sentence is called for. (By math sentence, I mean something that looks like math, such as an equation or a division problem.)

There are all kinds of stumbling blocks between the would-be solver and the solution to a math word problem. There could be reading problems, memory problems, calculation problems, problems with separating relevant from extraneous information. You will see in the following mini-lesson how one teacher uses visualization to get students to understand the heart of the problem.

Math

Mini-Lesson:
Mr. Eamon's Visualizing Math Word Problems Continued

"The hardest part about a word problem is figuring out what kind of math you need to do. Sometimes it helps to create a visual representation of the problem. It can be a drawing of what is going on, a table, Venn diagram, or any kind of pattern. This is good to do, because the time that you spend creating your visual is thinking time. It gives you space between your first reading of the problem (and that sinking feeling in your stomach), and your writing out the solution. Go ahead and draw some kind of visual that represents the problem."

Mr. Eamon waits for this to happen. "Okay, now explain your visual to someone else and listen to their explanation of theirs."

He listens, as the learning buzz fills the room. Then he asks, "Okay, now, who has a better understanding of what the problem is asking for?" He calls on volunteers to come up to the board, draw their visual, and explain their reasoning to the class.

Analysis

Manipulatives go hand-in-hand (literally) with visuals. Manipulatives concretize the problem, helping solvers to see how its words represent entities that are the same (named by different words) and those that are separate. For example, one problem is worded this way: "Five times a number is two more than ten times the number." Students must recognize that it is the same number that goes by the phrases "a number" and "the number." But such is not always the case.

Another problem is worded this way: "The sum of two numbers is 77. If the first number is ten times the other, find the number." Here, "the [first] number" signifies a different number from "the number" that we are to find. Visuals and manipulatives can help us sort this out.

Visuals and manipulatives are often overlooked as valuable math-learning tools in the upper grades, although elementary teachers know their effectiveness well. Although students won't have access to visuals and manipulatives on standardized, high-stakes tests, they can certainly cultivate the habit of mind of translating math verbiage into visuals to help them understand the language. Mr. Eamon, obviously sold on the value of visuals and manipulatives, requires that his students have all kinds of them: buttons, colored paper clips and push pins, paper money, Legos, Tinker Toys, Cuisinaire Rods, origami paper, algebra tiles, beads. He says, "My high school students love this stuff. They get very involved. The muscle memory and color-coded cues help them learn and remember. Visuals and manipulatives help them connect the abstract concepts to concrete objects. Math is *already* visual: the layout of the problems, the graphing, the tables. This only takes it one step further. It helps them to mediate the language."

The following are tips for teaching visualization and animation as a during-reading strategy:

- In literary text, the reader should always be able to answer these three questions:

  - Where is this taking place? If indoors, is it a private or public place? If a home, what room of the home? If outdoors, what kind of terrain is it?

  - Who is there?

  - What are the tensions?

- In science or mathematics text, where is the nearest illustration, and what does that illustration have to do with what I'm reading?

- A great deal of science text is about how things change. The reader should be able to picture the changes.

- In social studies text, the reader should form pictures of polarities: rich and poor, urban and rural, those in power and those trying to gain power, East and West, and so forth.

- In any text, the reader who has lost focus on meaning should refocus by looking for noun phrases that are easy to picture.

- Give the reader the idea of visualizing *more* than what is in the text. Remember that we experience the world with all five senses and supplement the text with other details to make it come alive.

- Provide as many visuals, including movies, of text as you can without eliminating the need to read. Think of the visuals that you provide as scaffolding, not replacement, for accessing meaning through text. Have the students match the words to the visuals.

- Have students create comic strips, using stick figures or bubble figures if they prefer, which represent their reading.

- Use visualization as a way for readers to understand organization by giving them the idea that they can create mental graphic organizers.

- You can never remind students enough that visualization and animation are strategies for creating meaning and refocusing as they read.

7

After-Reading Strategy: Taking Ownership Through Wrap-Up Activities

In this chapter, I'll show you several ways in which students can make their learning real to them after they've read the last words of their reading segments. The strategies that go into creating a wrap-up activity result in something that the teacher can assess. Thus, these activities serve the dual purposes of being learning strategies *and* assessments.

This is the after-reading strategy of taking ownership by engaging in some meaning-making activity such as conversation, creative dramatics, writing, or making a visual organizer. Traditionally, the only follow-up to reading that students did outside of class was a teacher-made quiz or test. The problem is, the students had to guess what was going to be on the test. Although many students are successful at the guess-what-you-have-to-remember assessments, such externally imposed experiences do little to improve the skills of deficient readers or, for that matter, improve the skills of competent ones.

If we begin to shift our thinking from the assign-test sequence into the guide-process-assess paradigm, we help students form the habits of mind necessary for success now and later. This does not mean that we forego testing students on their reading. But, we should be testing them only after we've gone beyond just telling them to read.

The mini-lessons presented in this chapter will be wrap-up activities, which purpose is to have students take direct, positive action after reading. Criteria for meaningful wrap-up activities are that they do the following:

♦ Represent a complete overview of the text, with the beginning, middle, and end of the text addressed.

- ◆ Develop students' independence as a learner. For this to happen, students must have some choice in what their wrap-up activity will be.

- ◆ Serve as a reference for future learning.

End-of-chapter questions provided by the textbook editors are only minimally acceptable as wrap-up activities because the student is likely to have little interest in them and thus not feel a sense of ownership over the answers. Such questions are fine as reading guides, for previewing, and for studying for comprehensive tests, especially summative assessments.

Keep it simple. You don't have to think up different wrap-up assessments for every reading task. Students can be given an array of choices, and these can even be given on a school-wide or certainly team-wide basis. The choices can be built around the major learning styles: verbal, visual, auditory, kinesthetic, tactile, social.

I'll use five components of reading comprehension as a guide for what should be included in a wrap-up activity: main idea, supportive details, vocabulary in context, inferences, and internal organization.

Wrap-Up Activities

Main Idea

Of course, the reader always has to express an understanding of the main idea, but we don't want the main idea to be stated too generally. I like the main idea to be stated as a substantial sentence. The sentence is substantial when the student could not have composed it without reading the text. For example, a student reads the chapter in the social studies text on checks and balances in American government. We don't want the main idea to be stated as, "It told about checks and balances in American government."

We *do* want the following:

"The Constitution is written so that the three branches of government check and balance each other so that one branch does not become too strong."

Or

"Each branch of government cannot become too strong because we have checks and balances in the Constitution."

Notice that each main idea statement has to meet several criteria:

- ◆ It states the main idea without wasting words about the fact that it is about to do so, as in "The chapter tells about…."

- ◆ It uses key vocabulary, such as *Constitution, branch of government, strong.*

- ◆ It expresses a relationship.

Supportive Details

In expressing comprehension of supportive details, the reader has to clearly link the details to the main idea. This can be done through an outline or other visual organizer, or through a traditional written paragraph. The student needs to show an understanding of the beginning, middle, and end of the text in the selection of supportive details.

Details given in text are not of equal importance. That is why outlines and graphic organizers are good forms to use for showing relative importance. Another good way for students to process relative importance of details is to have them decide which facts would be included in a test. Ask them to set up three columns as in Figure 7.1:

Figure 7.1. Detail Organization

Most Important (easiest, most general)	Moderately Important (fairly easy, somewhat specific)	Least Important (hard to remember, very specific)

Vocabulary in Context

Every reading experience should expand, reinforce, and/or refine vocabulary. Therefore, wrap-up activities should include a vocabulary component. Remember that vocabulary building is not limited to the learning of new words. It is also the learning of phrases and the development of new, clearer understandings of familiar or partially familiar language. Remember that every encounter with a word adds to our understanding of it until we are able to use the word spontaneously to express meaning. Vocabulary journals are especially useful when students understand that their understanding of language is dynamic, not static, and when they take into account how a word can change its form to adapt to different functions in a sentence.

Inferences

Wrap-up activities that call on readers to make inferences (draw conclusions) require them to go beyond the page. Applying the information to solve problems, identifying the assumptions of text, developing a feel for connotation and author's tone: These are activities calling for inferential thinking. Using the example of the text that describes the system of checks and balances in American government, we could have students draw inferences based on current events (text-to-world connection).

Making inferences is a high-level thinking skill involving knowing enough about the background of the text that we can read into it. Let's say, for example, that you are a fan of a particular baseball team, and you read an account of last night's game. Because of your prior knowledge, you could infer (draw conclusions) about how they might do in upcoming games against teams with certain strengths and weaknesses (you already know as background knowledge). If you had resources of background knowledge about the text on checks and balances, you could draw inferences about what the President, Congress, or Supreme Court might react to a situation that you follow in the news.

Your wrap-up activity will be shallow if it doesn't include inferences. Consider some kind of application, prediction, conclusion, connection, opinion, or judgment that brings the new information together with background knowledge to make inferences.

Internal Organization

Because you want students to be conscious of the organization of text as they read, you should include something in the wrap-up activity that addresses how the text is put together. It can be something very simple, such as a chart having the pattern clusters and asking the student to supply the page on which these pattern clusters appear, if they do appear.

Most informational text goes from general, to specific, and then back to general. Readers should be aware of this pattern and its deviations. For example, a newspaper article deviates from the general-specific-general pattern by presenting information in the order of descending importance. Most newspaper articles end with the least important information, without returning, as an editorial would, to the generality in the end.

I hope that your wrap-up activity will stand up to the following rubric as demonstrated in Figure 7.2:

Figure 7.2 Wrap-Up Activity Rubric

	Beginner	*Novice*	*Intermediate*	*Expert*
Understanding of main idea	No or minimal identification of main idea	Minimal or unsubstantial statement of main idea	Good statement of main idea	Clear, sharp, well-developed statement of main idea
Understanding of supportive details	No or minimal supportive details	Minimal or vague supportive details	Good identification of major supportive details	Clear, sharp, well-developed examples of supportive details
Understanding of vocabulary in context	No or minimal evidence of vocabulary growth	Minimal or incorrect use of new vocabulary	Good examples of vocabulary growth	Excellent evidence of vocabulary growth and/ or insight
Ability to make inferences	No, minimal, or incorrect inferences	Minimal or unsubstantiated inferences	Good inference (at least one)	Strong inferences
Understanding of organization	No, minimal, or incorrect understanding of how text is organized	Minimal or unsubstantiated text organization	Good understanding of how the text is organized	Full understanding of how the text is organized

Formative and Summative Reading Assessment

In case you don't remember from your undergraduate days, we speak of assessments as being formative or summative. Formative assessments are those that the student does along the way to meeting a long-term objective. Teachers are supposed to use formative assessments to determine instructional needs. Summative assessments are those that the student does at the end of a major time interval, such as a lengthy unit of study or a semester.

Reading Assessment

Example I: Social Studies

We are using comments about the Constitutional provisions for checks and balances fictitiously composed as if Thomas Jefferson were responding to the ideas of James Madison on the subject. Thomas Jefferson might say the following:

> "Well, my good and true colleague, Mr. Madison, has set forth a system of checks and balances between and among the three branches of government that would be in our new Constitution. Although I approve of Mr. Madison's checks and balances, still I fear that, under his plan, our federal government will prove too strong. As I've said before, I feel strongly that our new government should place as much power as possible at the state level, and as little power as possible at the federal level. After all, we fought a Revolution against the tyranny of a monarchy just so that our people could have more freedom from a highly centralized government."
>
> "Mr. Madison speaks of Shay's Rebellion. I believe that Mr. Madison has been unduly frightened by this event. After all, one has to expect occasional rebellion, and although the loss of life in a violent uprising is always to be regretted, we must remember that our new nation has experienced only one such rebellion out of all of our 13 states in the entire 11 years of our existence as an independent nation."
>
> "Coming back to our Constitution and how it should be written, I strongly suggest that it needs a Bill of Rights, and some other provisions to be complete. The people need to be protected from a standing army. The people need guarantees of freedom of religion and freedom of the press. On these freedoms, I feel that the federal government should stand firm regardless of the fact that our States already have guarantees for such freedoms."
>
> "I have one more point of disagreement with Mr. Madison, and it is an important one if our nation is to remain free. Mr. Madison advocates that the President of the United States may be elected many times, to serve again and again. I fear that if such reelection to terms of long service are allowed, then our nation may find itself once again under the thrall of a King." (Adapted from Abraham and Pfeffer, 1995)

Why a Student Might Have Difficulty Comprehending This Text

The language is accessible for the intended grade level here, but the reader would need background knowledge about the Constitution and the Bill of Rights and the difference in philosophies of founders Madison and Jefferson with regard to states' rights and the federal government. Indeed, the reader would have to put this piece in its historical perspective to comprehend its theme of how the Constitution should be crafted to organize the new nation. That is the thematic information. The specific information would be about Shay's rebellion. Without knowing what Shay's rebellion was about, the reader could deduce that the writer is talking about a violent uprising of the citizens against the government, which the government put down, not without loss of civilian life. Nevertheless, the ability to identify Shay's rebellion is assumed. Finally, the reader should understand Jefferson's use of the strong word *fear* in his defense of his position that the President of the United States serve not more than one term of office.

It is clear that the main necessity for the comprehension of this text is background knowledge, which should be provided in the before-reading mini-lesson.

A Wrap-Up Activity

Here are two wrap-up activities that the teacher could use to assess comprehension of this text:

1. Reverse Perspective: In this letter, Thomas Jefferson responds to the ideas set forth by James Madison. A good wrap-up activity would be to present the ideas of James Madison that prompted Jefferson's response. This could be done simply, point by point on a chart, or more elaborately, in the form of a speech or letter by James Madison. On an even more sophisticated level, the student could adopt the language style of the period.

2. Question and Answer: One way to understand this text is to see that it answers the main question: "What were the ideas that James Madison had about the Constitution that Thomas Jefferson disagreed with and why?" Answering this question point by point is an efficient wrap-up activity. You might want to have students pose the key question and then answer it, if you think they can extract that question from the text.

Example II: Latin

Let's take a look at the following sample text:

Nouns

In English and in Latin, a noun is a word that names a person, place, thing, idea, quality, or action. Nouns in Latin make changes in their forms to express the following: case, number, gender, and declension.

Case

A case of a noun tells you how it fits into its sentence. You will learn more about cases later on. To create the different cases in Latin, we change the ending of the nouns.

Number

The number of a noun means whether the noun is singular or plural. Nouns in English signify whether they are singular or plural also, usually by adding the -*s* ending. Many nouns in English signify that they are plural by other changes as well, such as adding -*es* (fox, foxes), or changing the *y* to *i* (lily, lilies), or the *f* to *v* (wife, wives). English has irregular plurals such as child, children; mouse, mice; deer, deer.

Gender

The gender of a noun tells you whether that noun is masculine, feminine, or neuter (neither masculine nor feminine). In English, inanimate nouns are neuter, and we refer to them as *it*. In Latin, every noun is either masculine or feminine.

Declensions

Declensions of nouns are not thought about in English. In Latin, we have five declensions, each category of declensions sharing the same ending to indicate its case. For example, in what we call the first declension, the nouns all end in -*a* in the nominative singular. Most nouns in the first declension are feminine.

To decline a noun, that is, to form its declension, we add the case endings to the stem, or base, of the word. We find the stem by dropping the -*ae* from the genitive singular form.

Why a Student Might Have Difficulty Comprehending This Text

This text introduces not only new facts (and new words for these facts, such as *declension*), but also the entirely new concept that languages other than English behave in all kinds of different ways from the way English behaves, that is, adding endings much more extensively than English does to enlist a word in a particular sentence function. I would assume that students reading this information would not be hearing it for the first time: You would have already taught this lesson about the nature of nouns in the target language, and the students would be reading this for clarification, as a review.

Still, the difficulty lies in the integration of the new language behaviors, which can be understood only in the context of the way that English behaves. So, cognitively, the student must absorb the following (although not receiving the information for the very first time):

♦ We're taking something that we know intuitively (English language) and analyzing it objectively. If the student doesn't really understand what a noun is, there's no way he or she can make sense of the information about noun behavior in the target language.

♦ We're understanding that not all languages behave the way English does.

♦ We're learning about different kinds of behavior of Latin nouns.

Wrap-Up Activity

This text definitely calls for a wrap-up activity that involves comparison/contrast. Here are three suggestions:

1. Use a Venn diagram to show the convergence and divergence of English and Latin in terms of noun usage. Students could make a separate diagram for case, number, gender, and declensions, or they could include all of these categories in a single diagram.

2. Write a paragraph explaining the differences and similarities between noun usage in English and in Latin. Such a paragraph would have to be heavy with the contrastive words *but* and *however.* More sophisticated students could learn to use the word *whereas* as a contrastive both at the beginning of and in the middle of sentences.

3. Create a two-column chart expressing how English and Latin use nouns for case, gender, number, declension.

Example: Science Text

How does a volcanic eruption affect wildlife?

> Five hundred and forty tons of ash exploded into the sky in 1980 when Mount St. Helens erupted in the state of Washington. Ash and fire flew down the mountain like a furious river. This river of fire generated so much heat that the air temperature elevated 35 degrees in ten minutes for a 35 mile radius.
>
> Every living thing within a six and a half mile radius from the eruption perished and was buried under six feet of ash and rocks. Fortunately, the people in the surrounding area were given ample warning to evacuate, and so the death toll among humans was kept to a minimum, considering the magnitude of the event. Loss of wildlife, of course, can only be estimated, but environmental scientists (forest rangers and biologists) presume that approximately 1,400 coyotes, 300 bobcats, 6,000 deer, 200 black bears, 5,200 elk, 11,000 snowshoe hare, and 15 mountain lions died in the aftermath of the St. Helens eruption.

Why a Student Might Have Difficulty Comprehending This Text

The information here is extremely concrete, and the language is accessible, so this text does not represent significant challenge to the reader who knows how to decode. However, the reader would have to perceive the intended purpose of this narrative within a living environment textbook. A multiple choice question for comprehension of purpose might look like this:

The author's main purpose in this passage is to:

1. express the cause and effect relationship between a volcanic eruption and the living environment.

2. call for greater protective measures to prevent loss of wildlife resulting from a volcanic eruption.

3. have the reader experience what a volcanic eruption looks like and feels like

4. tell a story about the eruption of Mt. St. Helens.

It's very important that the reader perceive that (1) is the answer to this question. Although the other choices are valid responses to the text, they are personal responses and not correct interpretations of the author's intent in the context of a living environment textbook. This is because cause-and-effect relationships, and not emotional or political responses to information, are central to scientific thinking, and scientific thinking is obviously what we're after in a science course.

It's tough sometimes to separate out what we experience as the most important idea to us personally from what we must assume to be the author's intent. Students sometimes cling to the notion that whatever they take from text is what they were intended to take. Although that can be true for literary text—and we could argue that point—it is not true for informational text, which has a much narrower window for personal interpretation.

Why, then, would a science text use dramatic language at all, if we are not supposed to respond emotionally? I'd say that the answer is that the use of the dramatic and descriptive language is motivational and interesting to the reader. But readers are still obliged to think like scientists when reading science, just as they must think like poets when reading poetry. It's all about genre expectations: knowing where you are and what's expected in that place.

Wrap-Up Activity

The science teacher wants the student to extract scientific information from this anecdotal text. Here are two examples of wrap-up activities that would accomplish this:

1. *Application:* Have the students describe a fictitious volcanic eruption, using a real volcano somewhere on the planet. In their descriptions, they should include the scientific information that they glean from this text. For variety, their description could be created in the form of warning to the populace surrounding the area to evacuate, giving details of what might occur in a volcanic eruption, and why. This activity would require research into the kind of wildlife in the area that they choose for their setting.

2. *Annotation:* The wrap-up activity could also consist of annotating a copy of the text in the margins. The annotations would identify the *results* of the volcano. For example, the annotation for the first paragraph could say: "Eruption results in lava flow rushing down mountain, raising temps by 35°."

Example: English Language Arts Text

> Our legions are brimful, our cause is ripe.
> The enemy increaseth every day;
> We, at the height are ready to decline.
> There is a tide in the affairs of men
> Which, taken at the flood, leads on to fortune.
> Omitted, all the voyage of their life
> Is bound in shallows and in miseries.
> On such a full sea are we now afloat,
> And we must take the current when it serves,
> Or else lose our ventures.

Why a Student Might Have Difficulty Comprehending This Text

Everyone, even Shakespearean actors, I'm told, has trouble comprehending Shakespearean text at some points. Students are usually overwhelmed by it, and many barely give it a chance before giving up. Although I am not in favor of turning any but the most sophisticated high school students out to read Shakespearean text for the first time on their own, I do favor explicit reading comprehension lessons on the readings done together in class. I also believe that reading Shakespearean text (as a group) offers the most valuable and comprehensive reading lessons that we can do in English classes.

Despite its reputation for being difficult, a great deal of Shakespearean text, such as this speech by Brutus in Act IV of *Julius Caesar*, is quite accessible on its face. Any difficulty in extracting meaning from this text is not because of the words or the syntax. But, the reader who thinks that Brutus is merely giving a navigational report would be, of course, not comprehending the meaning of this text.

I'll say that there are two blending streams of thought that unlock meaning in this text, which can be applied to other texts: The first is the understanding of motif, and the second, relatedly, is the understanding of metaphor. Without those understandings, the reader takes Brutus's speech literally and fails to grasp its significance.

Motifs, recurrent images that have significance to the story as a whole, serve the same purposes as any (other) kind of literary repetition: unity, emphasis, pattern. In this particular Shakespearean play, we find the motif of water, particularly the sea and its ability to change. In this speech, Brutus is talking about change and opportunity, using the metaphor of the sea, a metaphor that has been a motif throughout the

English Language Arts

play. So it is the recognition that the sea represents change, opportunity, and timing that is the key to accessing meaning in this bit of text. Comprehension requires a lesson in literary thinking.

Wrap-Up Activity

As with everything Shakespearean in the classroom, the text offers multiple opportunities for creative teaching. My least favorite approach to Shakespearean text is to have the students write a "translation" of the text into "modern English." Not only is this unoriginal and uninspiring, but, to me, it causes the students to go backward in their thinking, taking something rich and strange and reducing it to something mundane. For this text, I can suggest three wrap-up activities that can certainly be applied to other Shakespearean texts and that improve comprehension of literary text in general.

1. *Title-Making:* Ask students to find another phrase within Julius Caesar that could serve as a title for this speech, and ask them to briefly explain their choice. This wrap-up activity accomplishes three worthy things: (a) It gets students thinking about the main idea of the speech; (b) it gets them scanning the whole text, a reading skill in itself; and (c) it hones the skill of finding the kind of evocative language. Ever since the plays were written, it has been a great literary tradition to snip off bits of Shakespearean text and stick them on original creations to be used as titles. I think of titles as little marvels of word engineering, and title-making is a craft deserving attention for anyone interested in written communication.

2. *Choral reading:* A choral reading of Shakespearean text (or any poem) is a chant-like rendition of the text in which key words or lines are repeated in the background as a refrain by a kind of chorus, while a speaker, or group of speakers, recite it. In the case of this speech, it might sound something like this:

    Refrain: Take the current when it serves

    Take the current when it serves

    Take the current when it serves

    When it works as it should, the choral reading forms a kind of poetic, interpretive jazz-like improvisation that creates meaning through the group effort of blending text, rhythm, and voices. The choral reading can be done with the whole class, with small groups, or with just two voices.

3. *Making divisions:* Another good way of making meaning in Shakespearean text (or any poem) is to divide it into sections of meaning. You can combine the title-making with the divisions by having students designate a title for each section.

Example: Math Text

> A polynomial is **factored completely** when each of its factors cannot be factored further. Sometimes it is necessary to use more than one factoring method to factor a polynomial completely.
>
> Example: Factor $2x^3 - 50x$ completely
>
> *Solution:* $2x (x + 5) (x - 5)$

Why a Student Might Have Difficulty Comprehending This Text

A reader would have to know the domain-specific meanings of the mathematical terms *polynomial, factored, factor, factoring method.* It might help to translate the passive voice into the active voice, which would make the first sentence look something like this: *You factor a polynomial completely when you have exhausted all of its factors (you can't do any more factoring of the factors). You might have to use more than one factoring method to make this happen.*

Wrap-Up Activity

It would seem that the ability to do the problem would be the most efficient wrap-up activity; however, it might be possible to do the problem without having understood the text, either by getting lucky, or by using another method. Even though the correct answer is arrived at, we still want the student to comprehend the text because its information can be necessary to understand future concepts. Therefore, in addition to solving the problem, we might want the student to do a wrap-up activity. Here are three suggestions:

1. Rephrase the text by making different kinds of sentences that express the same meaning. (Do not rephrase mathematical language by replacing mathematical terms with ordinary language.)

2. Create a mathematical visual, such as a Venn diagram, flow chart, graph, or mathematical problem, which illustrates the principles that the text is trying to explain.

3. Create and solve a word problem that can be solved by the principle that the text explains.

Example: Social Studies Text

Read the following article that appeared on the front page of the New York Times *on April 6, 1968 and then answer the questions that follow.*

Khensanh, South Vietnam—The 76–day North Vietnamese siege of the Marine base at Khensanh was officially declared lifted today.

The United States marines and helicopter-borne Army troops today pushed toward what was described as North Vietnamese regimental headquarters south of the base.

The 20,000-man relief column reached the base and then fanned out on three sides in search of the vanishing enemy soldiers. Army helicopter units entered the base.

The sweep could take the Americans all the way to the Laotian border, less than 10 miles away, in an effort to root out the 7,000 men asked to remain in the enemy force once estimated at 20,000. North Vietnam uses Laos as a staging area for attacks along South Vietnam's borders.

The United Stated command said that helicopter gunships of the First Cavalry Division (Airmobile), crisscrossing the skies ahead of the ground troops, killed 50 North Vietnamese late yesterday near the town of Khesanh, which is two miles south of the base.

Earlier, United states troops fought about 10 enemy soldiers four miles east of the town. Nine enemy soldiers and one American were reported killed.

1. Write one sentence explaining what the article says happened at Khensanh on April 6, 1968.

2. What does the reporter presume the reader already knows about the conflict in Vietnam?

3. Does the article tell you anything about the opinions of the journalist who wrote it? Explain.

4. What is one source for some of the information contained in the article?

5. Might that source be biased in any way? Explain.

6. What would you like to know about the siege of Khensanh that is not in the article?

Social Studies

Why a Student Might Have
Difficulty Comprehending This Text

The main challenge in this text is that the reader has to understand military language. Almost every sentence has a word or phrase in it that has a literal or metaphorical military meaning. Of course, if the reader didn't know anything about the relationship between South and North Vietnam, or the relationship of the Americans to this region at this time, then the article could not be understood.

Would answering the questions provided in the textbook be a worthy wrap-up activity? The first question calls for encapsulation, certainly a worthwhile task. We'd want the student to paraphrase the first sentence. They need to express that they understand that the United States Marine base had been under attack (siege) for some 76 days and that the United States Army forces now drove away the North Vietnamese, who had been the attackers. The second question calls for the student to think about prior knowledge, also a worthy, strategy-based question. The third question asks for inference, or, in this case, lack of it. It asks us to notice that the language of the journalist is without bias or emotion. Because the ability to perceive author's tone and intent is an important reader's strategy, this question is also worthwhile. The fourth question is highly inferential, with the answer found in the sentence "The United States command said that…" That leads right into the expected answer to the fifth question that, yes, the source of this newspaper article might indeed have a motive for spinning the information in a particular way. And, the last question calls for continued thinking about the reportage of a military action.

Although, as I've stated, I'm not crazy about text-produced questions except as previewing strategies, these particular questions are actually quite good: They call for critical thinking and valid reading habits for social studies reading, where the perspective of the person telling us history must be taken into consideration.

Wrap-Up Activities for Special Learners

For English language learners and for students with special reading problems, the wrap-up activity can be a summary or the creation of a graphic organizer that summarizes key points. These are scaffolding activities that allow struggling students to extract basic knowledge through reading while on their way toward higher level skills.

In addition, I stress the importance of having such students keep a language journal in which they record new words and phrases that they accumulate through reading.

Summary

Finally, always keep your mind open for opportunities that allow students to tie their learning into their own culture. They are a different generation from you and me; they are inheriting a world in which information processing can be significantly different from the culture that we grew up in. (This applies no matter how young a teacher you are today!). They connect to images, music, and language that we don't even know about, much less think about.

Remember that wrap-up activities create the link between the known and the new. Don't think of them as superficial ways to memorize information, such as acronyms, jingles, or other rote memorization gimmicks. Such devices can serve their purpose for information that does need to be memorized, but we should devise wrap-up activities that have meaningful substance.

IV

Schoolwide Programs

8

What Works?
What Doesn't?

In researching the information for this book, I relied on the National Council of Teachers of English (NCTE). The NCTE's Commission on Reading sought out "sound, standards-aligned criteria to apply as [they] select[ed] program materials or design local programs of instruction in reading" (NTCE, 2006). Their researchers identified 110 features that could be present in a school's reading program. For each feature, they assigned a value from 1 to 4, with 1 being the least likely to result in the improvement of comprehension, and 4 being the most likely to improve it. The 1 to 4 rating system is detailed as follows:

- A rating of 1 means that this program feature is **not an important** feature for an effective literacy program.

- A rating of 2 means that this program feature has **minor importance** for an effective literacy program.

- A rating of 3 means that this program feature is **important** for an effective literacy program.

- A rating of 4 means that this program feature is **essential** for an effective literacy program.

What the NCTE suggests is that educators use this information as a basis for reflection and conversation: As we make decisions about how to teach reading, to what extent do our decisions comport with research about durable education? How can we move toward those features that receive a rating of 4 (essential for an effective literacy program)? What do we think we should do about those features rated 1 (not an important feature for an effective literacy program)? Might those features serve some other purpose, and, if we claim that they do, can we find serious research to support our practices?

The program features are divided into the following categories:

- Media/tools used to teach reading
- Scope of materials

- How students are grouped
- Instructional approaches
- Comprehension strategies
- Word recognition and word study
- Reading/Writing connections
- Student role
- Assessment
- Professional resources and development

Media and Tools Used to Teach Reading: What Works? What Doesn't?

On the feature of media and tools used to teach reading, the least effective features, those rated 1, are these:

- Decodable texts
- Skills-based texts
- Controlled vocabulary
- Publisher-substituted (as opposed to original) illustrations
- Recall-level worksheets

What all of these ineffective media and tools have in common is the *inauthentic* reading experience: The more we attempt to create text that is controlled for vocabulary and skills, the more we fail to improve comprehension.

Here are the media and tools that are rated with a 2, still ineffective, but a little better than the preceding:

- Abridged texts
- Leveled texts
- Videotapes
- Internet

What we have here lacks sufficient length and breadth for readers to develop stamina. These are pseudo-reading experiences, and they miss the mark when it comes to providing the full swim in literary waters that leads to truly improve reading comprehension.

Here are the media and tools that rate a 3:

- Computer software
- Audiotapes

The first, computer software, varies in quality, so I think it's hard to consign it to a particular level of effectiveness without knowing what kind of computer software is being matched to what kind of student. As for audiotapes, they at least offer the sound of real text, and are especially useful for those with emergent English-speaking skills.

Now, here are the media/tools considered the most effective in improving comprehension:

- Authentic connected texts, complete and unabridged
- Predictable texts
- Nonfiction texts
- Classroom libraries
- Original illustrations
- School-to-home connections
- Suggestions for extended readings

Reading Materials: What Works? What Doesn't?

The next category of reading program features deals with what the reading materials represent, their *scope*. On this set of features, the researchers list only those that deserve the highest rating, which are the following:

- Authentic multicultural perspectives (text and illustrations)
- Accurate, current information
- Wide range of purposes
- High literary quality
- Range of authors
- Multiple disciplines
- Multiple genres
- Content likely to engage and interest readers
- Content that is of interest to both genders
- Conceptual or thematic structures

Does the textbook that comprises most of the required reading in your class meet these criteria? If not, what can you do to provide an interesting variety of reading materials?

Grouping:
What Works? What Doesn't?

The next feature in the study had to do with grouping. "Fixed ability" groups came in with a 1 rating, with "pull out instruction" not far behind, getting a 2. Better results are to be had with "whole class" instruction, but the best results are achieved (rating 4) when we have small groups that are selected not for ability alone, but for ability *and* interest. Having students work individually also gets a high rating.

Instruction:
What Works? What Doesn't?

As for instructional approaches, which is the next set of features, you won't be surprised to know that "scripted, sequenced, teacher-directed" styles get a rating of 1, as do "strategies and skills taught in isolation." The latter might take the form of a "lesson on previewing" that is disconnected from actual text that is about to be read and is previewed right now. The instructional approaches receiving ratings of 3 are these:

- Role play
- Projects
- Guided reading
- Shared reading
- Partnered reading

Those earning a 4 are these:

- Student generated topics and questions
- Strategies and skills embedded in meaningful text
- Scaffolded instruction toward independence
- Discussion
- Extensive independent reading and free choice reading
- Literature study

Note, again, the importance of authenticity and autonomy where the individual's interests and needs are respected. As for the list of approaches designated as 3, it stands in their favor that they are constructivist (with active learning), but they (except, arguably, for role playing) respond to external prompts about what is to be learned and how. They are approaches that don't allow for as much freedom of thought as do the 4s. (And, by "literature study," the NCTE would favor a "reader response" model, where the reader creates meaning in the ground between reader and text, rather than the "formalist" model, where the teacher gives the one-and-only "right" interpretation.)

Teaching Comprehension Strategies: What Works? What Doesn't?

Under the set of features bundled as "comprehension," the researchers used only two designations, 1 and 4. There was a single 1 on the list, and it was this: "Emphasis on application of skills in isolated text excerpts." In other words, if you wanted to teach "previewing," you would not be wise to teach it against a specific paragraph chosen just because of its ability to be used for that skill. Rather, you would teach the skill of previewing because it would be useful for authentic text that lies in the student's natural path of reading material. Here are the highly rated (i.e., rating 4) program features for comprehension:

♦ Development of higher level thinking and critical literacy

♦ Emphasis on meaning making with connected text, including focus on using fiction and nonfiction text structures and features

♦ Multiple perspectives, themes, and interpretations

♦ Independence in learning (self-direction)

♦ Development of cognitive strategies (predicting, questioning, confirming, summarizing, inferring)

♦ Development of metacognitive strategies

♦ Support of risk-taking

♦ Development of multiple cueing systems (syntax, semantics, spelling, context, punctuation)

♦ Opportunities for comprehension work (before, during, after reading)

♦ Intertextuality (bridging from one text to another)

♦ Development of schema that connects new information to known information

Most of this book is about integrating these comprehension strategies as mini-lessons that immediately precede reading.

Teaching Word Recognition: What Works? What Doesn't?

The next category of program features addresses word recognition and word study. These are the program features at the lowest level (i.e., rating 1):

♦ Phonemic awareness in isolation

♦ Phonics in isolation

♦ Reading fluency without comprehension (read fast, don't understand)

♦ Decoding of pseudo words

♦ Word lists

And, these are the not-much-better 2s:

♦ Phonological awareness

♦ Vocabulary lists

Again, we're seeing the proven ineffectiveness of isolated bits of information. Connectedness is the key, as we see from the 3s:

♦ Phonemic awareness in context

♦ Phonics in context

♦ Etymological focus for vocabulary

♦ Vocabulary building with roots and affixes

As you can see, now we're moving toward meaning by going from isolation to context. Let's take that one step further, into the 4s:

♦ Alphabetic principle (the concept of the relationship between speech and print)

♦ Sight words (the ability to recognize a word immediately, despite the fact that it may not be spelled phonetically)

♦ Reading fluency with comprehension (read without interruption, understand)

♦ Miscues as window into cue and strategy utilization (e.g., "This is why I misread this word. This is how I can fix my mistake pattern.")

♦ Word families (e.g., "These words belong together for some reason.")

♦ Experiential base for vocabulary (e.g., "I learn a word because I need that word to communicate.")

♦ Vocabulary from text (I'm seeing the full context, not just a phrase or single sentence)

♦ Concept-driven vocabulary instruction (A new word represents a new concept, not just another label for an old concept.)

Reading/Writing Connections: What Works? What Doesn't?

Reading and writing enjoy a mutually beneficial relationship. The researchers considered ineffective and effective ways in which writing is used as a tool for strengthening reading comprehension. The least effective ways (rated 1 and 2) are these:

♦ Fill-in-the-blank as response to text

♦ Multiple choice responses to reading

♦ Essay writing

I listed the first two only because they were included in the report, but I can't say that I consider these "writing." The third, essay writing, surprised me for being rated a 2, and not higher. I'm assuming that the low rating owes to the inauthentic (prompted, highly structured) way in which essays are assigned: Students are not given open-ended questions that satisfy their own curiosity about the text, but are performing to external specifications.

The program features in the reading/writing connections category that get a 4 rating are these:

♦ Constructed spelling as approximation

♦ Spelling as a window into phonics knowledge

♦ Response to text in students' own words

♦ Reading and writing integrated, for example, text as source for student writing opportunities

♦ Discussions about individual and social uses of literacy

What we can conclude is that for writing to strengthen reading comprehension in the best way possible, we need to have students be *invested in* the writing task, and given some responsibility for using their knowledge (of spelling, for example) to create meaning. Keeping students in the narrow zone of right-or-wrong limited answers to pointed questions has little effectiveness or authenticity.

The Student's Role:
What Works? What Doesn't?

The next category of program features is "student role." The only feature rated as 2 in this category is "completion of reading logs," considered a low-level, rote skill. "Reading log" would be a slippery term. If the reading log were like a captain's log, a schedule of what was read when and maybe a few summarizing statements or shallow comments (e.g., "It was boring."), then we can see the shallowness. But if by "reading log" we mean something that is more like the dialectical (i.e., double entry) journal where the student records meaningful responses that show connections and predictions, then it would be far more useful as a comprehension builder. You'll see the phrase "process journal" following, as distinguished from a "reading log."

The "student role" program features awarded a 4 rating are these:

♦ Choice of reading selections

♦ Choice of reading extension activities

♦ Documenting and assessing reading growth via self-reflection, portfolio development, process journals, and so forth

♦ Increased independence and responsibility, such as social interaction around literacy, inquiry into own and others' literacy processes and practices, encouragement of risk-taking in reading and writing

Note the high degree of student involvement in bringing new information gleaned from reading into their own world to make meaning. Note also the importance of choice, not only in the selection of reading materials, but also in the response to it. In short, it's good to see that not everybody is doing the same thing (differentiated content).

Assessment:
What Works? What Doesn't?

Now we come to assessment. Assessment can be a thing apart from learning, or it can be a learning experience in itself. The former assessments, unit tests, and formal, standardized tests, receive a rating of 1. Multiple choice comprehension tests fare not much better, with a 2 rating. On the higher side, we have student-directed assessment (rating 3), and the following with a rating of 4:

♦ Classroom-based, ongoing (running record, miscue analysis, retelling, anecdotal observations, student reading histories, records of reading)

♦ Written reactions and responses to texts (but not prompt-driven essays)

♦ Portfolios

♦ Lists of learners' reading experiences

What these 4-rated assessment practices have in common is that they are based not on "snapshot views" of the student's ability to answer finite questions, but on professional observations made by a teacher who understands reading and who views assessment through a diagnostic paradigm.

Professional Resources and Development: What Works? What Doesn't?

The last program feature category is professional resources and development. Here, scripted programs receive a rating of 1. Receiving a rating of 3 are data on student outcomes and support for teacher research, for example, teacher inquiry topics and findings. The following are the features that receive a 4 rating:

♦ Support for meeting needs of individual students (resources, instructional approaches)

♦ Resources and professional development experiences to build teacher knowledge about learning and literacy

♦ Research and theory base of the program provided

♦ Support for teacher as instructional decision-maker

♦ Provision for parent education, support, and involvement

Why the Old Model Doesn't Work

You may remember when the paradigm for secondary school reading instruction was the remedial reading class wherein students would work on isolated skills one at a time, using bits of text that were unrelated to anything else that they were reading in school. Sometimes, these programs were *individualized*, with students coming into a *reading lab*, picking up folders and commercially prepared, sequenced *lessons* off a shelf. The lessons may have been color-coded for *levels*, and the student would proceed to *work through* the work through the series of skills, completing one level (color) at a time, stepping up to the next, working through the skills.

The skill series may have looked something like what follows: Main idea: Given a *passage* about the craft of making whale harpoons, the student answers multiple choice questions about its main idea. The questions might be phrased in the form of "the best title for this passage would be…," or "the main idea of the passage is…," and so on.

The other skills in the sequence may have been detail, inference, vocabulary in context, cause and effect. It is not that such skills as finding the main idea, identifying details, making inferences, using context clues to access word meaning, and perceiving cause and effect relationships are not essential reading skills. Of course, they are.

The ineffectiveness of such programs, as we now acknowledge, is the meaningless and artificiality of the reading experiences. The skills, assumed to transfer from the reading lab to the social studies class, did not necessarily do so. The multiple choice questions did not facilitate meaning. They just assessed whether the student could do those particular questions. Nevertheless, the program assessment for this kind of instructional paradigm was multiple choice questions!

The second problem with the "reading lab" programs just described is that they were given not to all students but only to those "needing remediation." But all students need to be instructed in reading strategies because all students will, sooner or later, encounter challenging reading material. And reading instruction should be a lively, social experience, not a dreary factory model of doing multiple choice question after multiple choice question about a hodgepodge of topics chosen for their ability to have multiple choice questions asked about them and not much else.

Summary

What you are looking for is the degree of presence of those program features deemed to be important (rating 3) or essential (rating 4). The NCTE Commission emphasizes that the point of the list of program features and their ratings is to generate conversation among colleagues, not to achieve a certain score.

Why certain program features get a higher rating than others is not a mystery. Highly rated features cluster around the following characteristics:

Authenticity: The readings simulate the kind of reading that real people do in real life.

Choice: Everyone appreciates having *some* control over their lives. Unmotivated students report that it is the lack of control over their lives in school that blunts their desire to achieve. Once you offer a choice, you involve the learner and increase the chances for success.

Immediate use: When time intervenes between the learning of a skill and its use, all kinds of connections are lost. A reading strategy is a tool. A tool has a purpose. When you learn how to use a tool, you need to try it out right away.

Engagement: Students need to talk, write, draw, question, and create to make meaning out of text. The engagement, to be most effective, needs to come from within, rather than having the only engagement be the answering of teacher, textbook, or state-generated questions.

Variety: We see the word *multiple* a lot: multiple genres, multiple voices, multiple kinds of pedagogy. We need to extend our reading offerings beyond the textbook.

Conclusion

I hope that after reading this book you've refined and maybe even reconstructed your understanding of what reading comprehension really is, how it works, and how you can intervene to help your students improve their skills in the context of your classroom. I hope you've seen that doing so results in enriched learning in your subject, not a distraction from your plans.

For students to learn through reading, they need to approach reading as a process, but they can need your assistance in guiding them through that process, consistently reminding them that reading is a process of before, during, and after mental activities that work together to extract meaning from text. Consistent, school-wide messages will eventually build in students the habits of mind to approach reading with a prepared mind, to read with focus and reread when necessary, and to continue to think about what they've read, engaging in a constructive activity to solidify meaning.

Reading comprehension depends on the accumulation of both knowledge and skills. Background knowledge and vocabulary growth are simultaneously necessary for, and the results of, the habit of reading. Vocabulary, syntax, and the visuals on the page are the ingredients that go into text, so students need to exist in an environment that is as rich as possible in the kind of academic language that comports with the language that they meet in reading academic text. Although the home and community can offer such language, many students do not derive familiarity with academic language anyplace else *but* the school. It is we who speak, write, and teach reading in that language.

What I've asked you to do here is to make an investment. I've asked you to believe that the time you spend teaching reading through the mini-lessons is time that you've spent teaching **your subject** in a way that will prove to be more efficient than the "teaching around reading" that you may have been doing. I hope that you will come to think of reading instruction as something that you *can* do without being a certified reading teacher and with positive results for how your students learn not only your subject but in extracting meaning out of text for anything that they want to learn.

The Strategic Reader

Before Reading		
What do I already know about this subject?	What am I reading to find out?	What do I know about the main ideas from previewing?

During Reading		
What are the main pattern clusters? Narrative/Description Classificatio Definition Example Cause & Effect Comparison/Contrast Process Analysis	How can I connect my life, other readings, and the world, today and in history, to this reading?	What am I visualizing and animating as I read?

After Reading		
What can I create, think about, talk about, or do that will help me make sense of and remember what I just read?		

References

Abraham, H., & Pfeffer, I. (1995). *Enjoying American History*. New York: Amsco.

Alabama Reading Initiative. (2003). *Secondary Training Manual*. Montgomery, AL: ALSDE.

Armstrong, T. (2003). *The Multiple Intelligences of Reading and Writing: Making the Words Come Alive*. Alexandria, VA: ASCD.

Beck, I., & Juel, C. (2000). *"The Role of Decoding in Learning to Read." Implementing the California Reading/Language Arts Standards Professional Articles on Instruction, Research, and Classroom Practice*. Austin, TX: Holt Rinehart and Winston.

Beers, K. (2000). *"Research, Reading, and Holt Literature and Language Arts: Meeting the California Reading/Language Arts Framework." Implementing the California Reading/Language Arts Standards Professional Articles on Instruction, Research, and Classroom Practice*. Austin, TX: Holt Rinehart and Winston.

Billmeyer, R., & Barton, M. L. (1998). *Teaching Reading in the Content Areas* (2nd ed.). Baltimore, MD: Association for Supervision and Curriculum.

Caine Learning Institute. http://www.cainelearning.com

Crow, J. (2005). Feeding Reading: Writing from an Information-Based Perspective. *NTCE English Journal, March*.

Hirsch, E. D., Jr., (2003). Reading Comprehension Requires Knowledge—of Words and the World. *American Educator, Spring*, 10–44.

International Reading Association. (1999). *Summary of adolescent literacy: A Position Statement for the Commission on Adolescent Literacy of the International Reading Association*. Washington, DC: International Reading Association, Inc.

Irvin, J. (2000). *"Content-Area Reading: Helping Students Become Better Readers and Better Learners." Implementing the California Reading/Language Arts Standards Professional Articles on Instruction, Research, and Classroom Practice*. Austin, TX: Holt Rinehart and Winston.

Jacobs, H. H. (2006). *Active Literacy Across the Curriculum: Strategies for Reading, Writing, Speaking, and Listening*. Larchmont, NY: Eye On Education.

Kenney, J. M., Hancewicz, E., Heuer, L., Metsisto, D., & Tuttle, C. L. (2005). *Literacy Strategies for Improving Mathematics Instruction*. Alexandria, VA: ASCD.

McWhorter, K. T. (2001). *Academic Reading* (4th ed.). New York: Longman.

Middleton, S. & Stokes, C. M. (1999). *The African American Experience: A History* (2nd ed.). Upper Saddle River, NJ: Globe Fearon.

Nagy, W. E. (1988). *Teaching Vocabulary to Improve Reading Comprehension.* Urbana, IL: NCTE.

National Council of Teachers of English (NTCE). (2006). Features of Literacy Programs: A Decision-Making Matrix. Available at http://www.ncte.org/about/over/positions/category/read/118620.htm.

Schoenbach, R., Greenleaf, C., Cziko, C., & Hurwitz, L. (1999). *Reading for Understanding: A Guide to Improving Reading in Middle and High School Classrooms.* San Francisco:Jossey-Bass.

Short, D., & Montone, C. (2002). *Integrating Language and Culture in the Social Studies Training Packet.* Washington, DC: Center for Applied Linguistics.

Tovani, C. (2000). *I Read It, But I Don't Get It: Comprehension Strategies for Adolescent Readers.* Portland, ME: Stenhouse.

Ullman, B. L., & Henderson, C., Jr. (2003). *Latin for Americans.* New York: Glenco McGraw-Hill.

Vacca, R. T., & Vacca, J. L. (1999). *Content Area Reading* (6th ed.) New York: Longman.

Zimmermann, S., & Keene, E. O. (1997). *Mosaic of Thought: Teaching Comprehension in a Reader's Workshop Cornerstone Project.* Portsmouth, NH: Heinemann.

Zwier, L. J. (2002). *Building Academic Vocabulary.* Ann Arbor: Michigan University Press.